INCLUSION:
A Service, Not A Place

A WHOLE SCHOOL APPROACH

REVISED EDITION 2012

Dorothy Kerzner Lipsky, Ph.D.
Director, Center on Educational Restructuring, Affiliated with The Graduate School and University Center, The City University of New York

Alan Gartner, Ph.D.
formerly Co-Director of National Center on Educational Restructuring and Inclusion (NCERI): currently Chief of Staff, Deputy Mayor for Education and Community Development, City of New York

PUBLISHING

A Division of
National Professional Resources, Inc.
Port Chester, New York

Publisher's Cataloging-in-Publication
(Provided by Quality Books, Inc.)

Lipsky, Dorothy Kerzner.
   Inclusion : a service, not a place : a whole school approach / Dorothy Kerzner Lipsky, Alan Gartner. -- Rev. ed.
   p. cm.
   ISBN 978-1-935609-58-2

   1. Inclusive education--United States.
2. Mainstreaming in education--United States. 3. Children with disabilities--Education--United States.
I. Gartner, Alan. II. Title.

LC1201.L558 2012   371.9'046'0973
                         QBI12-600053

Acquisitions Editor: Helene M. Hanson
Associate Editor: Lisa L. Hanson
Production Editor, Cover Design: Andrea Cerone,
National Professional Resources, Inc., Port Chester, NY

© 2012, Revised Edition, Dorothy Kerzner Lipsky

Dude Publishing
A Division of National Professional Resources, Inc.
25 South Regent Street
Port Chester, New York 10573
Toll free: (800) 453-7461
Phone: (914) 937-8879

Visit our web site: www.NPRinc.com

All rights reserved. No part of this book may be reproduced or transmitted in any form or by any means, electronic or mechanical, including photocopying, recording, or by any information storage and retrieval system, without permission in writing from the publisher, with this exception: pages intended for use as Blackline Masters, labeled on top left corner of the page with "BLM-," may be copied for classroom and/or staff development purposes, not for resale.

Printed in the United States of America

ISBN 978-1-935609-58-2

Dedication

For our grandchildren, who bring us enormous joy, laughter, and learning

Eleanor
Simon
John
Alexa
Drew
Henry
Charles
Spencer
Samantha
Tessa
Max

and their parents.

Acknowledgments

The authors are deeply grateful to the teachers and administrators in school districts across the country for all they have taught us.

The substantive input and editorial assistance of Helene Hanson is greatly appreciated.

As with all our work, at its base is the gift Daniel Lipsky has given us.

—DKL & AG

Table of Contents

Chapter 1   Introduction & Overview 1

Chapter 2   Education Laws 7
                  Blackline Masters # 1-8 29-41

Chapter 3   Developing a Student's Programs:
                  The Work of the IEP Team 43

Chapter 4   Collaboration 49
                  Blackline Masters # 9-10, and Co-Teaching Rating Scales 62-66

Chapter 5   Supplementary Aids & Services (SAS) in a Differentiated Classroom .. 67
                  Multiple Intelligences Table, Blackline Master #11,
                  Matrix of Instructional Strategies and Modifications,
                  and Inclusion Accommodations Chart 84-99

Chapter 6   Cooperative Learning, Peer Supports, Social Emotional Learning ... 101

Chapter 7   Interventions: Academic & Behavioral 113
                  Blackline Masters #12-14 133-135

Chapter 8   Technology, Including Universal Design for Learning 137

Chapter 9   Additional Resources
                       Supporting Print & Video Material 147-157
                       Organizations & Agencies 158-160
                       Glossary of terms 161-165
                       Endnotes 166-170

1
Introduction and Overview

This book is designed to serve as a hands-on, free standing implementation resource for teachers, general and special education. It may be used by teachers in their classrooms and/or as an integral part of the school or district professional development activities. It is also a valuable resource for undergraduate/graduate teacher preparation courses. While focusing on the work of those general and special education teachers who provide instruction, the book supports the roles of administrators, clinical personnel, and parents.

"Inclusion" (or "inclusive education") has become an all purpose phrase with little consistency as to meaning. In fact, the term does not appear in federal law. Karten (2011) provides a useful clarification distinguishing between "ideal inclusion" and "pseudo-inclusion." Examples of the latter include:
- assignments are standardized despite student differences;
- identical instructional goals, methods, and materials are given the entire class regardless of student differences;
- there are limited times when students with disabilities participate in age-appropriate activities with their non-disabled peers; and
- the general education teacher is the main instructor with the special education teacher in a permanent secondary role.

Distinguish "real inclusion" from a student with disabilities just being present. Necessary components of "real inclusion" include:
- students are in their home schools and general education classes in natural proportions, with needed supports and services;
- planning for inclusion is the starting point for all activities—academic, social and behavioral—and involves the full range of school personnel; and
- diversity is valued as a good in itself.

Looking at it from the perspective of parents, Sweden (2009) puts forth the following questions to ask of the school:
- are all students sitting together?
- are all students asked for responses and encouraged to participate?
- are there a variety of ways for students to participate?

- is there evidence of active learning?
- does each member of the teaching team express ownership for all students?
- are all students working in the same curriculum at varying levels of complexity?
- are students supporting each other?

While our focus is on benefits to students with disabilities, there are substantial opportunities for benefits for students without disabilities, including opportunities for meaningful friendships, increased appreciation and acceptance of individual differences, increased understanding and acceptance of diversity, respect for all people, preparation of all students for adult life in an inclusive society, and opportunities to master activities by practicing and teaching others.

Students with disabilities are first and foremost children, worthy of equal respect and opportunities, treatment, status, and place. A steady line of court cases affirm this as follows:

- Ronker v Walter (6th Circuit Court, 1993) established a principal of portability, ruling that if a desirable service currently being provided in a segregated setting can be delivered in an integrated setting, P.L. 94-142 would require that it be done so.
- Oberti v Board of Education (3rd Circuit Court), 1993) placed the burden for compliance with IDEA's mainstreaming requirement on the school system.
- Sacramento Unified School District v Holland (9th Circuit Court, 1994) held that the starting point for a student's placement was the "mainstream."
- Greer v Rome City Schools (11th Circuit Court) held that when a placement decision favored serving the student outside of the regular classroom, consideration must be given as to whether the student's needs could be met in the regular classroom with supplemental aids and services.
- Daniel R.R. v State Board of Education (5th Circuit Court, 1989) held that placement in a regular education classroom was a benefit in itself and could be provided even if it were not the best academic setting.
- Board of Education v Rowley, 2nd Circuit Court, 1982) required individualized decisions based upon the unique needs of each student.

To facilitate the use of materials compiled/developed by the authors, fourteen Blackline Masters (BLMs) are provided. These may be reproduced and used for classroom and/or staff development purposes. (See copyright information on the back of the title page). These BLMs are located at the end of the chapter in which they are referenced. Each reference includes the number of the BLM; e.g., BLM No. 4, and the page where it is located. These BLMs are contained within a heavy black border. Additional resource material is also included at the end of Chapters 4 and 5.

The content of this book builds upon the activities of the National Center on Educational Restructuring and Inclusion (NCERI) and its work with school districts (urban, suburban, and rural) and state education agencies across the country. NCERI's work includes professional development for school and administrative personnel to support the implementation of inclusion, research about inclusion "best practices" and the effects of its implementation, and dissemination and publication of material. The book derives from the experience of more than a thousand school districts throughout the nation. It draws upon the growing body of "best practices" that have been identified by practitioners and researchers.

In today's schools, diversity is manifested in all aspects of demography: race, ethnicity, religion, language, economics, sexual orientation, family situation, and student transiency, as well as disability. At issue for schools and classrooms is not the reality of difference, but what we make of it. As a nation, we are moving from glorification of the melting pot to an honoring of the mosaic. Or as Minow (1990) has said in discussing the "dilemma of difference," the shift no longer "makes the trait" (or disability) signify stigma or isolation but responds to the trait as an issue for the entire community."

The book begins with discussion of pertinent federal legislation. It then provides a "how-to" approach to the development of an Individualized Education Plan (IEP) for students with disabilities, and spells out the requirements for the education of such students. It helps teachers design programs that provide the mandated access to the general education curriculum, and it gives information on the classroom utilization of supplementary aids and services as well as participation in state- and district-wide assess-ments. In addition, the book provides a guide for regular education teachers to participate effectively in the development and implementation of the student's program.

The book supports the implementation of inclusive practices by presenting the following:
- a definition and description of the inclusive practice;
- the relationship of the practice to Individuals with Disabilities Education Act (IDEA);
- "best practices," based upon experience and current research;
- roles for school personnel, administrators, related services providers, and clinicians;

- roles for parents;
- Blackline Masters (BLMs) for use in staff development activities, or by teachers to help structure inclusive classrooms;
- references for additional treatment about each topic;
- additional information about resources, organizations, videos, Web sites; and
- a glossary.

Where can I find additional information (research, policy data) about inclusive education?

There is an ever-growing body of books, articles, and handbooks that document the research, policy, and implementation of inclusive education. They include the following:

Anderson, Winifred, Stephen Chitwood & Diedre Hayden. *Negotiating the Special Education Maze: A Guide for Parents & Teachers.* Bethesda, MD: Woodbine House, 1997.

Bauer, Anne & Glenda Brown. *Adolescents and Inclusion: Transforming Secondary Schools.* Baltimore, MD: Brookes Publishing Company, 2001.

Bunch, Gary. *Inclusion: How To.* Toronto, Canada: Inclusion Press, 1999.

Deshler, Donald D. & Jean B. Schumaker. *Teaching Adolescents With Disabilities: Accessing the General Education Curriculum.* Thousand Oaks, CA: Corwin Press, 2005.

Falvey, Mary A. *Inclusive and Heterogeneous Schooling: Assessment, Curriculum, and Instruction.* Baltimore, MD: Paul H Brookes Publishing, 1995.

Gore, M.C. *Inclusion Strategies in the Secondary Classroom.* Thousand Oaks, CA Corwin, 2010.

Gore, M.C. *Successful Inclusion Strategies for Secondary and Middle School Teachers: Keys to Help Struggling Learners Access the Curriculum.* Thousand Oaks, CA: Corwin Press, 2003.

Halvorsen, Ann.T. and Neary, Thomas. *Building Inclusive Schools.* Upper Saddle River, N.J., 2009.

Halvorsen, Ann T. & Thomas Neary. *Building Inclusive Schools: Tools and Strategies for Success.* Boston, MA: 2001.

Hehir, Thomas. *New Directions in Special Education.* Cambridge, MA: Harvard University Press, 2005.

Karten, Toby J. *Inclusion Strategies and Interventions.* Bloomington, IN. Solution Tree Press, 2011.

Karten, Toby. *Inclusion Succeeds with Effective Strategies* (laminated reference guide). Port Chester, NY: Dude Publishing, 2009.

Karten, Toby J. *Inclusion Strategies That Work!: Research-Based Methods for the Classroom.* Thousand Oaks, CA: Corwin Press, 2004.

Kluth, Paula, Diana M. Straut, & Douglas P. Biklen. *Access to Academics for All Students: Critical Approaches to Inclusive Curriculum, Instruction, and Policy.* Mahwah, NJ: Lawrence Erlbaum Associates, Inc., 2003.

Kugelmass, Judy W. *The Inclusive School: Sustaining Equity and Standards.* New York, NY: Teachers College Press, 2004.

Lipsky, Dorothy K. & Alan Gartner. *Inclusion and School Reform: Transforming America's Classrooms.* Baltimore, MD: Paul H. Brookes Publishing, 1997.

Lipsky, Dorothy K. & Alan Gartner. *Standards & Inclusion: Can We Have Both?* (Video). Port Chester, NY: National Professional Resources, Inc., 1998.

McGregor, Gail & R. Timm Vogelsberg. *Inclusive Schooling Practices: Pedagogical and Research Foundations.* Baltimore, MD: Paul H. Brooks Publishing Co., Inc. 1998.

National Association of State Directors of Special Education (NASDSE). *Response to Intervention: Policy, Considerations, and Implementation.* Alexandria, VA: NASDSE, 2005.

Nolet, Victor & Margaret McLaughlin. *Accessing the General Curriculum: Including Students with Disabilities in Standards-Based Reform.* Thousand Oaks, CA: Corwin Press, 2000.

Norlander, Karen. *What Educators and Parents Need to Know about Special Education* (laminated reference guide). Port Chester, NY Dude Publishing, 2009.

Norlander, Karen. *RTI Tackles the LD Explosion: A Good IDEA Becomes Law* (DVD). Port Chester, NY: National Professional Resources, Inc., 2006.

Rief, Sandra. *Section 504: Classroom Accommodations* (laminated reference guide). Port Chester, Dude Publishing, 2011.

Robinson, Viviane & Mei K. Lai. *Practitioner Research for Educators.* Thousand Oaks, CA: Corwin Press, 2006.

Sailor, Wayne. *Creating A Unified System: Integrating General and Special Education for the Benefit of All Students* (Video). Bloomington, IN: Forum on Education, 2004.

Sailor, Wayne. *Whole-School Success and Inclusive Education: Building Partnerships for Learning, Achievement, and Accountability.* New York, NY: Teachers College Press, 2002.

Scull, J. and Winkler, A. *Shifting Trends in Special Education.* Dayton, OH: Thomas B. Fordham Institute, n.d.

Sweden, B.L. *Signs of an Inclusive School: A Parent's Perspective on the Meaning and Value of Authentic Inclusion,* Teaching Exceptional Children Plus, 5 (3) January 2009.

2
Education Laws

Introduction
Prior to 1975, federal legislation gave neither direction nor did it provide mandates for the education of students with disabilities, then designated as "handicapped." Federal legislation was limited to capacity building, personnel development, and research.

In 1975, with the passage of P.L. 94–142, "The Education for All Handicapped Children Act," the federal government established the right of "handicapped students" to a free appropriate public education (FAPE). (A decade later, the law was retitled, IDEA, "Individuals with Disabilities Education Act"). Prior to the passage of P.L. 94–142, the availability of education for students with disabilities differed from state to state, even from school district to school district. Variations included availability of services as well as whether parents had to pay for services. The 1975 law made explicit the public responsibility regarding FAPE to all, regardless of the nature or severity of the students' disability. Indeed, it may be said that the smallest word in the law's title, "all," is the most significant. Further, this education was to be provided in "the least restrictive environment."

In late 2001, "No Child Left Behind (NCLB)," was passed and IDEA was reauthorized in 2004. Together these two pieces of federal legislation strengthen both accountability and responsibility for the education of students with disabilities.

In an article heralding the thirtieth anniversary of the passage of IDEA, *Education Daily* wrote:

> The goal to include all students in general education is not without its challenges. But with NCLB's introduction of accountability for all students, and IDEA's emphasis on more meaningful inclusion for all students with disabilities into regular classrooms, many view it as inevitable. (August 11, 2005, p.1).

In January 2011, the US Department of Education Office for Civil Rights issued a special guidance defining which students should get special services under federal laws. The "guidance" addresses accommodations that would help students be on an even footing with their peers. These so-called "504 plans" are likely to increase substantially the number of students who qualify for disability-based help.

Looking at both laws, John Hager, assistant secretary, Office of Special Education and Rehabilitative Services, US Department of Education, points to a breakthrough toward full inclusion of students with disabilities. "Attitudinal: Going from no expectations to low expectations to increasingly greater expectations and what we have with No Child Left Behind to full expectations." (Education Daily, August 11, 2005, p.6)

Table 1 provides highlights of commonalities between IDEA and NCLB.

Table 1
Commonalities Between IDEA and NCLB

	IDEA	NCLB
High standards for all students	X	X
Testing for all students	X	X
Progress for all students	X	X
Quality teachers for all students	X	X
"Best Practices" (i.e., research based interventions)	X	X
Staff development	X	X
Flexibility in the use of funds (i.e., for both general and special education personnel)	X	X

One of the many efforts to connect the two laws is a recent publication of the Congressional Research Service, "The Education of Students with Disabilties: Alignment between the Elementary and Secondary Education Act and the Individuals with Disabilities Education Act." The report focuses on four broad policy issues within both laws (standards, assessments, accountability and teachers) that potentially create differing expectations or requirements for schools and teachers educating students with disabilities. Similar issues occupy the work of Title I/IDEA Working Committee, a joint initiative between the National Title I Association and the National Association of State Directors of Special Education.

As the two laws have been reauthorized over the course of the decade of the 2010s, the integration of the two has been a constant theme. While the proposal of some to replace the two with a single omnibus law is unlikely to occur in the near future, common approaches and programmatic features accelerate.

Two other laws warrant mentioning:
- Section 504 of the Rehabilitation Act of 1973 is a civil rights, anti-discrimination law to protect persons with disabilities from discrimination due to their disabilities.

- The Americans with Disabilities Act of 1990 (Continue as per text through "under "under IDEA and NCLB.

(For details, see Norlander (2011) and Rief (2010). Although protected under these statutes, there is much more assistance for students with disabilities under IDEA and NCLB.

IDEA (2004): What does the law require?
Since 1975, when P.L. 914–142, "The Education for All Handicapped Children Act," was passed, the nation's landmark special education law has been successively revised. The original law was far-reaching, guaranteeing to all handicapped children the right to a "free appropriate public education" (FAPE). Successive amendments over the following two decades extended the law, adding categories of disability, expanding the age of entitlement, and refining parental due process rights.

While a goal of IDEA is to ensure that all children with disabilities who are in need of special education services are identified ("Child Count"), so, too, it is a goal of IDEA to reduce the number of children unnecessarily classified as disabled. This goal is furthered by the provisions for a multi-disciplinary evaluation, including student (and parent) due process rights, as well as provisions for "prevention," i.e., services for students while they are served in a general education setting, including a Response To Intervention ("RTI") provision that allows districts to use up to 15% of their IDEA funds for early intervening services.

While the national "Child Count" reports for past years show a decline in IDEA Part B enrollment, identification of students of color remains disproportionally high, especially those categorized as with learning and behavioral difficulties. (In contrast to these categories, which rely on clinical judgment, the disproportionality is less in those categories which are based on biologically verifiable conditions, such as deafness or visual impairment.)

Pro-inclusion educators have dubbed the acronym "IDEA" as the Inclusion and Development Education Act, in recognition of the myriad of ways the 1997 reauthorization was supportive of inclusive education initiatives. These mandates, which remain in the 2004 amendments, include:

- bases for determining whether a student has a disability and is in need of special education services;
- process of, and participants in, the development of a student's IEP;
- factors to consider in determining a student's placement;
- participation of students in regular state and district assessments; and
- formula to be used in a state's funding of local districts for the provision of special education services.

P.L. 108–446 (IDEA 2004), enacted in the last days of 2004, builds on these mandates of the 1997 amendments, extends them, and connects this special education law with general education law, No Child Left Behind (NCLB), signed into law in early 2002. For example, while the 1997 IDEA amendments require that states' performance goals be "consistent, to the maximum extent appropriate, with other goals and standards for children (i.e., non-special education students) established by the state," the 2004 amendments change this to require that states' performance goals "are the same as the state's definition of adequate yearly progress [per NCLB, see below]."

To understand the full meaning and consequence of the laws for students with disabilities, the following are good resources:

- regulations as issued by the U.S. Department of Education. On August 14, 2006, the U.S. Department of Education published the official final IDEA regulations for Part B. Those regulations went into effect in mid-October, 2006.
- policy guidance directives from the U.S. Department. There are frequent directives from the Department of Education regarding the interpretation of NCLB. Most pertinent are accountability and performance assessments for students with disabilities, and the interpretation of the "highly qualified" teacher requirement for teachers of students with disabilities.

Goals of IDEA

To achieve the inclusionary and accountability goals of the IDEA, the laws mandate the following:

- enhanced content of the Individualized Education Program (IEP);
- inclusion as the norm unless there is specific justification for a student not to participate with nondisabled students in academic, extracurricular, and nonacademic activities;
- provision of supplementary aids and services;
- involvement of a regular education teacher at the student's grade level in the development of the IEP;
- professional development for regular and special education personnel involved in providing services for students with disabilities;
- state funding formulas that are "placement neutral": ones that do not promote or encourage placement of students in more restrictive settings; and
- students with disabilities to participate in general state- and district-wide assessments, with needed accommodations and modifications.

The education program for students with disabilities must:
- address the general curriculum, not a separate special curriculum;
- provide the program in the regular education classroom, where the general curriculum is the norm, unless otherwise justified;
- identify the needed supports to enable the student to make progress in the general curriculum;
- be designed by a team including a professional familiar with the general education curriculum, e.g., a regular education teacher at the child's grade level, who is to be provided professional development to play this role;
- be funded by the state in a manner that does not encourage separate services;
- assess student learning per the general state- and district-wide program, with needed accommodations and modifications for the individual student with disabilities.

IDEA's requirement is that students with disabilities have beneficial access to the general curriculum. The law defines the "general curriculum" as that required by each state for students in general education. The requirement is mandated regardless of the student's placement. Those who provide instruction in either general or special education settings must know the general curriculum. Several provisions of the law address engaging students with disabilities in the general curriculum. The following are three important factors:
- the IEP: In the development, review, and revision of a student's program (i.e., the IEP), a regular education teacher at the student's grade level must participate with the other members of the IEP Team. This is to be the case for all but a few students, where a prior decision, reached with the parents' involvement, has been made that the student will not participate in the regular education environment.
- personnel: All personnel involved in the student's education, regular education teachers and special education staff, teachers and related services providers, must be informed of their responsibility to implement the student's IEP and the specific accommodations, modifications, and supports that must be provided for the student;
- resources: Funds are available to school districts to provide professional development to regular and special education teachers in serving students with disabilities.

The IEP is the primary tool
The IEP is the primary tool for ensuring the student's involvement and progress in the general curriculum. To achieve this, the IEP must:

- describe the present level of performance: this includes how the student's disability effects her/his involvement in the general curriculum; the presence of a disability is not warrant alone for exclusion from such involvement;
- specify measurable goals: the student's progress in the general curriculum must be measured, at least annually, against a set of clearly defined, measurable goals;
- identify services: the student's special education and related services, and supplementary aids and services needed to support involvement and progress in the general curriculum, are to be identified; and
- specify supports for school personnel: the student's program must specify the supports which enable school personnel to promote student progress in the general curriculum and participation in extracurricular and nonacademic activities.

As the US Supreme Court said in Schaeffer v Weast (2005), "The core of the statute [IDEA] is the cooperative process that it establishes between parents and schools... The central vehicle for the collaboration is the IEP process. The collaboration runs the full gamut of the student's involvement. Parents are full members of the IEP team.

Parents may initiate a referral for evaluation (or re-evaluation), must consent to the evaluation, are entitled to see the evaluation, may withhold consent for student classification and placement (both initial and change), are entitled to revoke consent for provision of services under IDEA, as well as entitled to pursue a range of due process procedures." (For details regarding the development of the IEP, see the following chapter.)

Goals of No Child Left Behind (NCLB)
Signed into law in January 2002, No Child Left Behind is both the most recent and most extensive revision of the Elementary and Secondary Education Act, originally enacted in 1965. Its hallmark is the requirement of accountability or results for all students. As part of state and school district responsibility and accountability for all students, including those with disabilities, NCLB requires:
- reporting achievement data disaggregated for student groups based on poverty, race, and ethnicity, disability, and limited English proficiency;
- setting state standards in reading, science, and math;
- testing of *all* students annually in grades 3–8 and at least once in grades 10–12; and
- establishing annual statewide progress goals to ensure that all students reach proficiency within twelve years. In assessing students with disabilities, accommodations must be provided.

Where the IEP team determines a student cannot participate in the state assessments (students with the most significant cognitive disabilities, defined as those whose intellectual functioning and adaptive behavior is at or below three standard deviations below the mean), even with accommodations, alternative assessments must be provided.

As part of the law's focus on outcomes for students with disabilities, with the narrowest of exceptions, NCLB requires:
- standards be set;
- curricula be developed;
- assessments be undertaken; and
- accountability be established (reflected in adequate yearly progress, "AYP") that is the same, or aligned with, the state's standards, curricula, assessments, and accountability for students in general.

Regardless of the resolution of the current dispute as to what percentage of special education students should be able to demonstrate proficiency in reading, mathematics, and science through alternative or modified assessments, and thus enable a school to meet its adequate yearly progress (AYP) standard, at least 97% of the students are to be held to the general education standard.

For students in districts and schools that fail to make adequate yearly progress toward statewide proficiency goals, including students with disabilities, there is a sequence of measures, including "public school choice," where FAPE must be provided, as well as supplemental education services, that are consistent with the student's IEP.

As part of its focus on teacher quality, NCLB requires the following:
- teachers be trained to teach and address the needs of students with different learning styles, particularly students with disabilities;
- special education teachers teaching core academic subjects must meet the "highly qualified" requirements; and
- rigorous standards for paraprofessionals working with students with disabilities be established.

As this manual goes to press, substantial modifications to the content and implementation of NCLB are underway; these will involve significant consequences for the education of students with disabilities, including provisions for inclusion. So, too, with IDEA.

The presumption of an inclusive environment
Since the initial passage of P.L. 94-142 in 1975, the Least Restrictive Environment (LRE) concept has been a part of the federal law. Neither the term "inclusive education" nor the word "inclusion"

appears in the law; however, education of a student with disabilities with her/his nondisabled peers is the presumption, unless specifically rebutted. Special education is considered a service, not a physical place.

The 1997 IDEA sharpened the provisions of previous laws by requiring that in the development of a student's IEP there must be specific justification of a decision for a student not to participate with non-disabled peers in academic, extracurricular, and non-academic activities. This justification must be particularized, subject area by subject area, and involves all of the activities of the school, the entire academic curriculum, clubs, sports, after-school activities, and student transportation. Prior to proposing exclusion, the IEP Team must have considered the benefits of related services and modifications or supports for the student and/or school personnel. "IEP Team" is the term that the federal government uses for the group that determines whether a student is disabled, based upon IDEA's specification of categories of disability,[1] and in need of special education services. If the student is in need of special education services, the IEP Team then develops the program of services. Members may vary from state to state, as does the name of the team; for example, some states use the term "Committee on Special Education," others "Child Study Team," and still others, different terms. This book uses IEP Team as the generic term.

Provision of supplementary aids and services (SAS)
The term supplementary aids and services, specified in the law, is often confusing to teachers and administrators, as they initiate a "whole school approach" to inclusion.

"Supplementary aids and services" for a student and her/his teacher(s) are the tools or help that is needed to enable students with disabilities to gain benefit from their involvement with the general curriculum. The focus in this book is on the provision of supplementary aids and services to support a student's participation in academic activities. Equally, the law requires the provision of such aids and services to support a student's participation in non-academic and extracurricular activities. This includes all clubs and after-school sports and activities. The law and its requirement regarding supplementary aids and services applies to all of the activities conducted by the school district; it is in effect, 24 hours a day, 7 days a week. Illustrative of the range of this effort is the following report: "Around the country, an increasing number of educators argue that school districts should provide more integrated transportation for students with special education programs."[2] The report notes that "school districts have started using innovative methods to conquer what some call the final frontier for inclusion—the bus ride."[3] These methods include equipping some full-size buses with wheelchair lifts, pairing students with disabilities and nondisabled students to ride on the bus together, having aides ride the inclusive regular bus, and using all size buses for all groups of students. Also suggested is including bus drivers at meetings that craft a student's program.

For the most part, the supports used by teachers in regular classrooms for students with disabilities are appropriate for all students. With this being the case, the supports that teachers find successful for students without disabilities make the participation of the student with disabilities more natural. One of the most common statements made by teachers in inclusive classrooms is that, "Good teaching is good teaching is good teaching."

Teacher Reported Supplementary Aids and Services
Among the range of supports that teachers report as most effective in an inclusive classroom are the following:
- collaborative teaming and consultation;
- team teaching;
- curriculum adaptations;
- environmental accommodations;
- building friendships;
- cooperative learning;
- classwide peer support activities;
- inclusion facilitators;
- heterogeneous grouping for instruction;
- study skill training;
- use of technology; and
- alternative instructional strategies (e.g., differentiated instruction, multi-sensory instruction, small group instruction, heterogeneous grouping for instruction).

The classroom teachers must consider the effects for both the class as a whole and the student(s) with a disability.

The support should:
- maximize student participation and interaction;
- enhance the respect and dignity of the student;
- promote independence;
- build on the learner's strengths;
- increase the student's self-esteem;
- be generalized across school and community settings; and
- benefit all students.

The concept of "least intervention needed" cautions the service prescriber that too much help may be harmful, both unnecessarily costly and potentially becoming disabling help.

When the focus is on the concept of *least intervention needed* (rather than LRE) and the concept is approached first from the perspective of need, the primary concern is not about placement. [Moreover,] the focus is not just on the individual but on improving environments. [As a result] many problems that now require special education can be prevented...

Regular education teacher participation in IEP development

Historically, a student's IEP had been developed by special educators, including both evaluative and pedagogic personnel. Congress has recognized the importance of the participation of a regular education teacher at the student's grade level in the development of the student's IEP. As the goal is the student's involvement and progress in the general curriculum, it becomes essential that someone familiar with that general curriculum be involved in the design of the student's program. The only exception to this requirement is if a prior decision has been made that the student will not be served in the general education environment. School districts are increasingly recognizing that such an important decision should be made as part of the IEP development and not prior to it and are including a regular education teacher as a matter of routine. This process supports a school district, should litigation be brought by parents at a future time.

While the requirement of the regular educator presents scheduling issues for schools, his/her presence has several important benefits. These include:

- ensuring that the IEP addresses the actual content of the grade's general curriculum;
- offering the opportunity for the regular education teacher to identify the supplementary aids and services needed to support the student's progress in the general curriculum; and
- providing the opportunity for the teacher to identify the supports she/he might need in order to enable the student to make progress.

The IEP Team meeting presents a unique opportunity for a regular education teacher to have her/his professional development needs addressed. Should a support be recommended for a student by the IEP Team and the teacher not be familiar with it, then the teacher may request professional development to learn the new skill/practice, or support by a specialist, such as a psychologist, social worker, reading specialist, or another teacher. For example, should a behavior management program be required for a student, the classroom teacher can request assistance in developing and implementing a behavior plan. As part of a student's IEP, providing support to a teacher becomes an obligation of the school district.

Professional development for general education personnel

IDEA replaces the model of students with disabilities receiving services only in special education classes from "special educators." Instead, given the goal of involvement and progress in the general curriculum, regular education personnel are to be integrally involved in the education of most students with disabilities, both in the program design and its implementation. Each of a student's teachers and other service providers, special and general education, must be informed of their role in implementing the student's IEP, including the specific accommodations, modifications, and supports that must be provided. The rules concerning confidentiality of student records do not preclude the informing of all school personnel involved in a student's program, nor is ignorance of the provisions of the IEP a basis for failure to implement it.

In recognition of the training needs of all staff, the law authorizes the use of IDEA personnel preparation funds to support the professional development of general education personnel. The law requires that each school district disseminate information on promising educational practices to all staff, including general and special education teachers, support staff, and administrators. In addition, the law requires that districts adopt such promising practices.

"Placement neutral" funding

Prior to the passage of the 1997 IDEA amendments, the Congress found that in nearly all of the states the funding of local school districts for special education services encouraged more restrictive placement; at the same time the law required services in less restrictive settings. While the percentage of state funding for local districts varies from state to state, the national average of state funds provided was about fifty percent of the local cost of special education.

IDEA now requires each state to establish a "placement neutral" funding formula that does not encourage more restrictive placements. As IDEA's funding increases over the years, the new funding will be allocated based upon the overall number of students in a school district (sometimes called "census-based" funding), rather than the current system that provides a "bounty" for labeling students.

It is expected that this change in state funding formulas, along with the changed basis for new funding, will encourage school districts to sustain students in general education settings rather than place them in more restrictive special education settings. The funding changes can provide more "prevention" services for all students in general education without requiring a special education label prior to the intervention. Based on this shift in the federal law and state practices, many schools are now providing services within general education that had previously been defined as special education. These services may include speech/language services as well as counseling, and physical and occupational therapy. Providing services in a more natural setting for all students and offering the opportunity for these services without children being labeled can be a great benefit for the whole school. For the school district, it means eliminating expenses in conducting unneeded evaluations and having additional funds to provide a greater extent of "prevention" services.

Services provided to students with disabilities may also benefit non-disabled students; this is a consequence of the revocation of the "incidental benefits" rule. For example, effective instructional design and feedback procedures as part of an individualized behavioral intervention plan for a given student with a disability may have benefit for the class as a whole. The provision of IEP-prescribed resources or related services in the general education classroom, sometimes called "push-in" services, may serve to benefit all students, including those who are not disabled.

Participation in state- and district-wide assessments

Since the goal for students with disabilities is involvement and progress in the general curriculum, the law provides for assessing the learning of students with disabilities through general state- and district-wide assessments.

The supplementary aids and services in instruction are to be provided to enable the student to make progress in the general curriculum and should be parallel to the accommodations and modifications that are to be provided in the assessment process. Such accommodations and modifications are not to be limited solely to district- and state-wide assessments; they are to be integrated into classroom instruction. The implementation of supplementary aids and services in instruction and accommodations and modifications in assessment enable a student to demonstrate her/his knowledge to the classroom teacher, and provide the student with familiarity with the accommodation and modification, when it is used on the district- and state-wide assessment.

Accommodations and modifications are designed to enable students with disabilities to demonstrate what they know; this minimizes the influence of the impairment on the outcome to be measured. One can conceptualize three types of accommodations and modifications as related to assessment:

- mode of assessment, e.g., extra time given for the student to complete the test, a different location for the test;
- format of the question, e.g., use of Braille rather than printed text, larger print, reworded questions, questions on tape or read to the student; and

- format of the answer, e.g., use of other than a "bubble" answer sheet, answers dictated or recorded.

The federal requirement does not specify the precise nature of the accommodations and modifications to be provided for students with disabilities. As states and districts implement this requirement, issues of test reliability and validity are being raised. As "high stakes" tests are increasingly used to determine grade-to-grade promotion and high school graduation, the application of accommodations and modifications only for students with disabilities presents a set of concerns about standards and validity. IDEA asserts that for students with disabilities schools set "high expectations and ensure their success in the general curriculum." In measuring the progress of students with disabilities, it is the student's learning that is to be the focus, not the manifestation of the disability.

What is a "whole school" approach?

The importance of a "whole school" approach is expressed by the Congress in the reauthorized IDEA. The law says that the education of students with disabilities will not be enhanced by "tinkering" with special education; rather, what is called for is a systematic and systemic approach. The school as a whole is expected to be a place where special education services are provided, and these services are to be provided in the context of the school as a unit. Special education is no longer to be considered a place to which students are sent; it is a service or group of services which students receive, across all activities of the school. Providing services to students with disabilities in the general education environment increases the likelihood that "prevention" or enhancement can be provided to nondisabled students without labels.

Central to the changes in IDEA is the expectation that intervention must begin before a student fails. The basic "whole school" approach involves strengthening the overall educational program, so that all classrooms provide a basis for effectively educating a wider range of students. In a school characterized by an inclusive education approach, there will be:

- MORE experiential, inductive, hands-on learning,
- MORE active learning,
- MORE emphasis on higher order thinking and learning of key concepts and principles of a subject,
- MORE in-depth study of a smaller number of topics,
- MORE responsibility transferred to students for their own learning,
- MORE choice for students,
- MORE enhancing and modeling of the principles of democracy,
- MORE attention to affective needs and the varying cognitive styles/intelligences of the students,

- MORE cooperative, collaborative activity, among both students and teachers,
- MORE heterogeneously grouped classrooms, where individual needs are met,
- MORE provision of help in the regular class setting,
- MORE varied and cooperative roles for teachers, parents, administrators, and community members, and
- MORE reliance upon teacher descriptive evaluation of student growth.

At the same time, there will be:
- LESS whole-class, teacher-directed instruction,
- LESS student passivity,
- LESS classroom time devoted to fill-in-the-blank worksheets, dittos, workbooks,
- LESS teacher focus on "covering" large amounts of material in every subject area,
- LESS rote memorization of factors and details,
- LESS stress on competition and grades,
- LESS "tracking" or leveling of students in "ability groups,"
- LESS use of pull-out programs, and
- LESS use and reliance upon standardized tests.[4]

Schools across the country have developed a variety of general education intervention formats, involving groups of general and special educators, and using such terms as "Teacher Assistance Teams," "Pupil Personnel Committees," "Child Study Teams," etc. Regardless of the name or the particular composition of the group, the goal and purpose of the effort is to marshal the full range of the school's resources, and to provide services to the students and the teachers in the general education environment. To attain greater success for students and teachers, schools need to use "best practices" and to create an on-going problem-solving environment that engages the full range of resources.

IDEA 2004 permits LEAs to use up to 15 percent of their Part B funds for early intervening services for students not identified as disabled.

The introduction of Response To Intervention (RTI) has the potential of providing necessary support to students experiencing learning difficulties. Using a tiered system that provides increasingly intense and targeted interventions, RTI holds great hope for early interventions that will mitigate continued learning difficulties for many struggling students. See Chapter 7 for more information on RTI.

The **Blackline Masters Nos. 1, 2, 3,** pages 29-33, may be used in a whole school approach to inclusive education, to determine goals, attitudes, and professional development needs.

How to get started with a "whole school" approach?

Inclusive schools and school districts are at different places in their implementation of a "whole school" approach that incorporates special education as a service in general education. While the federal law provides the framework within which all schools and districts must operate, there are many variations in how schools initiated the changes. According to the NCERI national study of greater than a thousand school districts, these include: a school board decision, an administrative directive, teacher initiative, parent discussion or court case, and a university (or other) funded project. Regardless of the initiation point, school districts have identified four common successful activities in the implementation process. They need not be used in a tightly prescribed sequence but can be viewed as key activities in developing a "whole school" approach to inclusive education. Information on these four activities follows.

1. Develop a district policy and a school mission statement

The "whole school" approach presented in the reauthorized IDEA suggests that a district policy concerning inclusion, and a school mission statement, should not be free-standing documents. They should be developed consistent with the practice of the district/school and be viewed as a part of the district and school overall design. If the practice in the district is for policies to be developed by a board of education committee that includes members of the community, a similar practice should be followed here. If the development of a school mission statement involves administrators, teachers, and parents, that should be the practice followed for this activity.

2. Inform parents and community

Parents and other community members need to be informed about IDEA and NCLB and consequent school changes. It is best for parents to become actively engaged at the school level. The overall tone in describing the inclusive education program should be in keeping with the school/district's approach to informing parents and community of any other change, as in the introduction of a new curriculum, a new grade organization, etc.

While there are separate program and placement issues that require the involvement of parents of students with disabilities as part of the IEP process in regard to their child(ren), parents of non-disabled students also need to have information about the school/ district policy and changes in the school mission and activities. The first general parent meeting should be convened by the principal, with other staff participation as appropriate. Among the topics for the meeting(s) are the following:

- explanation of the background for the change,
- its grounding in federal and state law, as well as district policy,
- the experience nationally and locally that demonstrates benefits for all students, disabled and nondisabled, and
- description of the steps and schedule of implementation at the school.

Written material to supplement the oral presentation should be available. Pilot efforts in the school or district can be presented by teachers and parents, and often are an effective method for transmitting information. Opportunities to visit programs, in the district or nearby, or to see a video, should be made available.

The **Blackline Master No. 4,** page 34, "Questions That Parents Often Ask," may be completed by the school/district and then used at meetings for both parents of general and special education students.

3. Establish a school planning group

Prior to the initiation of any significant program change, all groups in the school should be represented in the planning process. This includes: general and special educators, classroom personnel at the various grade levels/subject areas, related services and other support personnel, administrators, and parents. If the school already has a school leadership team, or similar group that is widely representative, it would be appropriate to use (or build upon) this organization.

While it is not essential that the principal be the chair of the group or participate on a meeting-by-meeting basis, it is essential that the school leader is active and supportive. Additionally, it should be made clear that the planning will have a direct effect on the entire school and is not a special education activity. For staff not directly involved in the work of the planning group, arrangements should be made to keep them regularly informed of the group's activities and progress.

4. School Self-Assessment

The initial work of the planning group is to conduct a school self-assessment. After the data is collected and analyzed, the planning group should move to developing a school plan and timeline for implementation.

Questions for the Planning Group: Developing a "Whole School" Approach
The following questions can serve as a guide for the school self-assessment.
a. *Why have students been referred for special education services in the past year? What supports in general education have kept*

students from being referred for separate special education services?

In examining referrals for special education or of students "at risk" and served without a special education referral, a cluster of needs is likely to emerge. In the NCERI study, districts across the country reported that referrals clustered in three groups: failures in reading and mathematics instruction, issues of discipline and student behavior, and matters of student family and home life. Often appearing were clusters at particular grade levels, especially at grade three or four, when the curriculum became more complex and/or external testing began. The purpose of the referral analysis is to determine what additional (or alternative) resources and programs could be established in general education to support students and enable them to remain and succeed in the regular classroom. The analysis is not to preclude students from receiving special education services, when needed. Rather, its purpose is to identify which broad services and programs are needed in general education and which become a part of the basic school program to reduce the need for special education referrals and services.

b. *What is the design of the current special education program?*

Examining the design and organization of the school's current special education services and program makes it possible to identify how services are organized, the number of students served in special education classrooms (i.e., outside of the general education setting), in general education classrooms, and the staffing of those classrooms. To serve all of a district's students in their home school, the school which they would attend were they not identified as having a disability, would move a district toward natural proportions of students, disabled and nondisabled. This would enable students to attend school with their siblings, friends, and neighbors. The personnel staffing special education classes as well as out-of-classroom personnel represent resources for the planning group to consider as they explore the (re)deployment of staff to enable the school to provide needed supports for students with disabilities in regular education classrooms. Collaborative teaching or other models of classroom support are discussed in Chapters 4 and 5.

c. *What practices/procedures in general education support/inhibit an inclusive school environment?*

In examining school practices, the separation between general and special education programs and services may emerge and will warrant examination. Whatever their appropriateness in the context of a separate special and general education system, separate practices may inhibit the development of a unitary system. Different student registration procedures, separate rosters, differing procedures for ordering of texts and other materials, separate evaluation of pedagogic personnel, are each examples of practices that reflect separation and mitigate against an inclusive school environment.

The **Blackline Master No. 5,** pages 35-36, "School Self-Assessment Guide: Practices in General Education that Support or Inhibit an Inclusive School," can be used to develop a comprehensive school plan.

d. *Which students presently served in more restrictive settings would benefit from special education services provided in the general education classroom with needed supplementary aids and services?*

Teachers in self-contained classes and others knowledgeable about the students in restrictive settings should review each student to identify what supports could be provided in general education classrooms. This is the first step in a process that will culminate in the IEP Team, including the parent, considering a change of placement.

Teachers of general education inclusive classes surveyed in the NCERI study report that their students, disabled and nondisabled, are more alike than different. They report that on standard outcome measures, the scores of students with disabilities would more likely be distributed than to be clustered at the lowest level. This finding should encourage an expansive approach to the consideration of students for participation in the general education classroom. In keeping with the ethos of IDEA and NCLB, this consideration should be undertaken focusing not on the student's disabilities nor on how she/he would perform in the class as it is currently conducted; rather, the consideration should be based upon how the student could perform with needed supplementary aids and services.

e. *What are the professional development needs of the school staff?*

The needs of staff for professional development will vary, by role as well as prior training and experience. In the needs assessment phase of developing the school plan, it is impor-tant to be specific and to offer teachers the opportunity to identify their professional development needs without fear of being labeled as incompetent. Some teachers may want to learn more about alternative instructional strategies or curricular modifications and others may want to learn more about the content of the general curriculum. And the process of collaboration may need to be learned by all staff. Clinical personnel may want to learn strategies for working in classrooms, with students and in support of teachers. Related services providers may want to learn about how to integrate their services within the regular classroom program.

Some professional development needs will be common across some or all of the schools in a district or among all staff in a particular role; in such instances, district-level professional development activities may be warranted. For the most part, however, professional development should be building-specific. In conducting professional development activities an underutilized resource is the expertise of the members of the school staff. The practice of teachers observing, coaching and/or mentoring has been demonstrated to be very effective. In a team teaching model, professional development takes place between the collaborators. When two teachers with areas of expertise work together and share their knowledge, the outcomes are positive for both professionals. (See Chapter 4.)

The **Blackline Master No. 6,** page 37, "Professional Development: A Self-Assessment Guide," may be useful.

5. The school plan

The plan should provide the basis for the school to become a quality inclusive school where, for the most part, services for students with disabilities are provided in general education classrooms. The design of a whole school approach to the education of students with disabilities is the culmination of the self-assessment activities, data collection, and its analysis. The planning group should avoid what has been called the "paralysis of analysis." In general, several months is sufficient time to conduct the school self-assessment and develop an inclusive building plan to present to the school staff and parents.

The plan should be specific and include a time frame for the implementation of its components. It should address:

- the general and special education needs of the students to be served;
- profile of school staff;
- professional development activities based on needs assessment;
- program models to be used;
- organizational and scheduling changes that are necessary; and
- evaluation of program and student outcomes including NCLB's required Annual Yearly Progress (AYP).

The process of adopting the plan will vary district-by-district. Whatever the particular procedures, this process should include sharing with parents and community, informing the entire school staff, and determining the consequences of the proposed changes on school-district relationships.

While the provisions of the laws provide the frame for inclusive education, a number of programmatic components are factors in success. These include:

- neighborhood school placement;
- natural proportions of students in the classroom (e.g., presumption that all all students are in a general education classroom);
- no segregated space, neither curricula nor extra-curricula;
- ongoing planning;
- creative teaching;
- a problem solving mindset;
- access to integrated after-school activities; and
- commitment to make it work.

The **Blackline Master No. 7,** page 38, "School Plan: Issues to Consider," may be used to develop the whole school approach.

6. Evaluating outcomes

A school must develop a way to assess and measure the outcomes of the implementation of the building's plan, and to use it to provide the basis for ongoing change.

Along with standard measures of student outcomes, the school planning group should address how they will measure the following issues:

- what are the effects for all students, in academic, behavioral, and social areas?
- what are effects for all staff in terms of enhanced school capacity; this includes staff professional development, new organizational models/ practices, (re)deployment of personnel, and classroom practices?
- What are the numbers of students previously served in special education classrooms in or outside of the home school building that now are being served in the home school? In general education classes with needed supports?

The **Blackline Master No. 8,** pages 39-41, "Quality Indicators of an Inclusive Environment," based upon NCERI's work with school districts across the country, as well as a review of the research literature, can be used in the planning process, and later as a review of progress made and as a monitor of implementation.

Where can I find additional information on the federal laws?

The basic sources of information are the laws themselves, IDEA and NCLB, and the regulations for their implementation. Full text of both can be found on the web as follows: www.ed.gov/IDEA and www.ed.gov/NCLB. Copies can be found in most public libraries and are available from the US Department of Education, Washington DC, 20202. Each state has a federally-funded Parent Training and Information Center (PTIC), which provides material for parents and others about the law. The PTICs can be contacted through each state's education department.

Details on IDEA (2004) are presented in "Individuals with Disabilities Education Act (IDEA): Analysis of Changes Made by P.L. 108–446," prepared by the Congressional Research Service, The Library of Congress. While issued on November 2004, *The Intersection of the IDEA and NCLB,* prepared jointly by the National Education Association and the National Association of the State Directors of Special Education (and published by the NEA), remains a valuable source of guidance.

Burrello, Leonard, Carol Lashly & Edith E. Beaty. *Educating All Students Together: How School Leaders Create Unified Systems.* Thousand Oaks, CA: Corwin Press, Inc., 2001.

Deiner, Penny Low. *Resources for Educating Children with Diverse Abilities, 4th Edition.* Florence, KY: Thomson Delmar Learning, 2004.

Downing, June and Snell, Martha E. *Including Students with Severe and Multiple Disabilities in Typical Classrooms.* San Francisco, CA: Paul H. Brookes Publishing Co., 2008.

Downing, June E. *Including Students with Severe and Multiple Disabilities in Typical Classrooms, 2nd Edition.* Baltimore, MD: Paul H. Brookes Publishing, 2001.

Gore, M.C. *Successful Inclusion Strategies for Secondary and Middle School Teachers: Keys to Help Struggling Learners Access the Curriculum.* Thousand Oaks, CA: Corwin Press, 2003.

Halvorsen, A.T. and Neary, T. *Building Inclusive Schools: Tools and Strategies for Succes.* Upper Saddle River, NJ, Pearson, 2009.

Harry, B. and Klinger, J. *Discarding the deficit model,* Educational Leadership, 64 (5), 16-21.

Hehir, T. *New Directions in Special Education.* Cambridge, MA: Harvard Education Press, 2005.

Jorgensen, C., Nisbet, J.A., and Schuh, Mary C. *The Inclusion Facilitators Guide.* San Francisco, CA: Paul H. Brookes Publishing Co., 2005.

Katzman, Lauren I. & Allison G. Gandhi (Editors). *Special Education for a New Century.* Cambridge, MA: Harvard Educational Review, 2005.

Kennedy, Eugene. *Raising Test Scores for All Students: An Administrator's Guide to Improving Standardized Test Performance.* Thousand Oaks, CA: Corwin Press, 2003.

Kugelmass, Judy W. *The Inclusive School: Sustaining Equity and Standards.* New York, NY: Teachers College Press, 2004.

Lipsky, Dorothy K. & Alan Gartner. *Inclusion and School Reform: Transforming America's Classrooms.* Baltimore, MD: Paul H. Brookes Publishing, 1997.

Moll, Anne M. *Differentiated Instruction Guide for Inclusive Teaching.* Port Chester, NY: Dude Publishing, 2003.

National Association of State Directors of Special Education (NASDSE). *Response to Intervention: Policy, Considerations, and Implementation.* Alexandria, VA: NASDSE, 2005.

Nolet, Victor & Margaret McLaughlin. *Accessing the General Curriculum: Including Students with Disabilities in Standards-Based Reform.* Thousand Oaks, CA: Corwin Press, 2000.

Norlander, Karen. *RTI and the LD Explosion: A New IDEA Becomes Law* (Video). Port Chester, NY: National Professional Resources, Inc. 2007.

Norlander, K. *Section 504 of the Rehabilitation Act: Students with Disabilities* (laminated reference guide). Port Chester, NY: Dude Publishing, 2011.

Norlander, K. *What Educators and Parents Need to Know About Special Education Law* (laminated reference guide). Port Chester, NY: Dude Publishing, 2009.

Rief, S. *Section 504: Classroom Accommodations* (laminated reference guide). Port Chester, NY: Dude Publishing, 2010.

Sailor, Wayne. *Creating A Unified System: Integrating General and Special Education for the Benefit of All Students* (Video). Bloomington, IN: Forum on Education, 2004.

Sapon-Shevin, M. *Widening the Circle: The Power of Inclusive Classrooms.* Boston, MA: Houghton Mifflin, 2007.

Schwarz, P.S. *Special Education: A Service, Not a Sentence.* Educational Leadership, 64 (5), 39-42.

The New IDEA: CEC's Summary of Significant Issues. Arlington, VA: Council for Exceptional Children, 2004.

Villa, Richard A. & Jacqueline S. Thousand. *Creating An Inclusive School, 2nd Edition.* Alexandria, VA: Association for Supervision & Curriculum Development, 2005.

Wright, Pam & Pete Wright. *Wrightslaw: From Emotions to Advocacy—The Special Education Survival Guide.* Hartfield, VA: Harbor House Law Press, Inc., 2001.

Wright, Peter W. D., Pamela Darr Wright & Suzanne Whitney Heath. *Wrightslaw: No Child Left Behind.* Hartfield, VA: Harbor House Law Press, Inc., 2003.

BLM No. 1

EFFECTIVE TEACHING PRACTICES:
A SELF-STUDY GUIDE

School practice and research findings report for classrooms to be effective teaching and learning environments, they must address lesson and classroom issues. The following presents examples of "best practices." Looking at your teaching practices, give an example of how you have used any of the following:

Lesson—

- A focus on district/state standards

_____

_____

- Content, materials, and resources that are appropriate to the needs of *each* student

_____

_____

- Clear expectations, connecting this learning experience to previous learning

_____

_____

- Models, guided practice, and varied opportunities for students to demonstrate mastery

_____

_____

- Ongoing assessment opportunities, including specific criteria for success

_____

_____

- Opportunities for students to work with and support one another

_____

_____

- Meaningful extensions, applications, and homework assignments.

_____

_____

Classroom—

- Posted examples of students' work, both in progress and completed.

_____

_____

(continued on next page)

BLM No. 1 (continued)

- A library of high-interest books, at different reading levels, available for students to use as resources and to read at home and in school.

- A variety of resources to use in projects, classroom instruction, and activities.

- Displayed information that reflects the students' backgrounds (reflecting diversity in terms of race, gender, culture, language, disability, and sexuality), and interests.

- Models, rubrics, and other information that assist students in their learning.

- Technology to support student learning, including higher order activities.

- Daily and weekly classroom schedules, highlighting any changes to the normal routines.

The classroom as a learning environment—
- Posted classroom and school rules and procedures.

- Clear expectations regarding appropriate student participation and behavior.

- A clear hierarchy of positive and negative consequences for various behaviors.

- Guidance and instruction in appropriate behavior.

Inclusion: A Service, Not A Place, by Dorothy Kerzner Lipsky and Alan Gartner.

BLM No. 2

FEATURES OF AN EFFECTIVE SCHOOL: A SCHOOL-STUDY GUIDE

School practice and research findings report that for schools to be effective teaching and learning environments, they must address schoolwide issues of curriculum, instruction, and staffing. The following presents examples of "best practices." Give an example of how each area was addressed.

- How the school instructional program is developed in the context of standards and assessment, which incorporate a range of curricula offerings and a variety of instructional strategies.

  _____

  _____

  _____

- Alignment of curriculum, instruction, and assessment

  _____

  _____

- Staff diversity, and the provision of professional development and support

  _____

  _____

  _____

- Collaboration among school staff

  _____

  _____

  _____

- Programs of student empowerment, including peer learning programs, active learning opportunities, and student-to-student support activities

  _____

  _____

  _____

- Family and community involvement in the school

  _____

  _____

  _____

(continued on next page)

BLM No. 2 (continued)

- Access to community and agency services, to serve students and to support school staff

  _____

  _____

  _____

- Schoolwide approach to behavioral issues, with shared expectations, standards, and consequences across all settings

  _____

  _____

  _____

- Presence of a regular system of accountability that defines success by the learning of each and all students

  _____

  _____

  _____

- A system of transitional supports from school level or setting to new level or setting

  _____

  _____

  _____

- Ongoing assessment and evaluation of student learning in the context of identified schoolwide goals

  _____

  _____

  _____

- Program of general education supports or interventions* that address student needs in the regular education setting

  _____

  _____

  _____

*The term "general education supports or interventions" is preferred to the more commonly used terms of "pre-referral," which suggests that this is a necessary step prior to a special education referral, or "prevention," which suggests that special education may be some sort of a disease.

Inclusion: A Service, Not A Place, by Dorothy Kerzner Lipsky and Alan Gartner.

BLM No. 3

QUESTIONS FOR TEACHERS: GENERAL EDUCATION INTERVENTIONS

Interventions in the general education program make the classroom a more effective learning environment for a wider range of students. Identify and give an example of:

- Modified classroom structure or physical arrangement

_____
_____
_____

- Adapted curriculum

_____
_____
_____

- Alternative curricula approaches and/or instructional strategies

_____
_____
_____

- Classroom positive behavior support program

_____
_____
_____

- Specialist services to support whole class learning. (e.g., reading or literacy specialists, guidance counselors, remedial specialists, related services personnel, nurse or other health services providers)

_____
_____
_____

- Needed services for parents of the students in my class

_____
_____
_____

- Supports made available to students with disabilities and provided in the general education class, per the IEP.

_____
_____
_____

Inclusion: A Service, Not A Place, by Dorothy Kerzner Lipsky and Alan Gartner

BLM No. 4

QUESTIONS THAT PARENTS OFTEN ASK

- What are the education reasons for the district/school offering a different model of services/programs for students with a disability? _____

- What does the federal law (the reauthorized IDEA) say? What does it require of our district? Of our school? _____

- What has been the district's experience in implementing IDEA? What has been the experience elsewhere in the state? The nation? _____

- What are the steps toward implementing IDEA? How will staff be prepared? How will outcomes be assessed? How will parents be informed of the outcomes? _____

- Will my rights as a parent be the same? _____

- Will the changes benefit students with disabilities at the expense of nondisabled students? _____

- Will including students with disabilities in regular classrooms overwhelm the teacher? Water down the curriculum? Slow up the learning of other students? _____

- Will the nondisabled students learn inappropriate behaviors? _____

- Will students with disabilities be able to obtain the special services they require in regular classes? _____

- Will children with disabilities be teased? Ostracized? _____

- What will happen to the staff, general and special education? _____

- How will the parents of children with disabilities relate to the additional school staff serving their children? _____

- Will the district's/school's budget be impacted? _____

- Will confidentiality be ensured? _____

Inclusion: A Service, Not A Place, by Dorothy Kerzner Lipsky and Alan Gartner.

BLM No. 5

SCHOOL SELF-ASSESSMENT GUIDE: PRACTICES IN GENERAL EDUCATION THAT SUPPORT OR INHIBIT AN INCLUSIVE SCHOOL

Whatever the appropriateness of particular school organizational and administrative practices in the context of a separate special and general education system, such practices may inhibit the development of a unitary system. For each of the following, consider the general practice and then address whether there are differences between special education students/staff and general education students/staff. If so, consider the rationale and continued appropriateness of such differences.

- How are registers set?

  General education: _____

  Special education: _____

- What are class size limitations?

  General education: _____

  Special education: _____

- How are student/teacher schedules set? For core subjects? For specials?

  General education: _____

  Special education: _____

- How are funds allocated?

  General education: _____

  Special education: _____

- How are other resources (e.g., textbooks, workbooks, computers, supplies, etc.) allocated?

  General education: _____

  Special education: _____

- What are reporting lines?

  General education: _____

  Special education: _____

- What are the lunchroom practices, e.g., location and time?

  General education: _____

  Special education: _____

(continued on next page)

BLM No. 5 (continued)

- What are the patterns of supervision?

    General education: _____

    Special education: _____

- How is classroom space allocated? Other facilities?

    General education: _____

    Special education: _____

- How is pedagogic staff assigned? Support personnel?

    General education: _____

    Special education: _____

- What are the school hours?

    General education: _____

    Special education: _____

- When does the school day begin/end?

    General education: _____

    Special education: _____

- What are the practices regarding extracurricular activities? Is transportation available? Are needed adaptations provided?

    General education: _____

    Special education: _____

- Are parents of all students eligible for membership in the school's parent-teacher organization(s)? To hold office?

    General education: _____

    Special education: _____

Inclusion: A Service, Not A Place, by Dorothy Kerzner Lipsky and Alan Gartner.

BLM No. 6

PROFESSIONAL DEVELOPMENT: A SELF-ASSESSMENT GUIDE

This questionnaire is part of our school self-assessment and is being used to identify professional development needs. The following are important practices in an effective classroom with general and special education students. Please identify areas of professional development which you feel would strengthen your classroom and our school. Also, please identify areas where you can offer assistance or training.

Check as many as apply

Classroom Practice	I would like professional development in this area	I can offer professional development in this area
Alternative assessment		
Alternative instructional strategies		
Assessment accommodations & modifications		
Assistive technology		
Collaboration		
Collaborative instructional planning		
Cooperative learning		
Curricular adaptation		
Differentiated instruction		
Multi-media instruction		
Paraprofessionals in the classroom		
Peer support programs		
Positive behavior support		
Preparation of general education teachers to participate in IEP meetings		
Provision of related services into classroom instruction		
Social integration/skill development		
Student self-management		
Study/test taking skills		
Supplementary aids & services		
Teaching/learning strategies		
Team teaching		

Name (Optional) _____

Inclusion: A Service, Not A Place, by Dorothy Kerzner Lipsky and Alan Gartner.

BLM No. 7

SCHOOL PLAN: ISSUES TO CONSIDER

There are many components of a school plan that promote inclusive education. In the context of districtwide policies, your school plan should address the following components:

- a philosophy that articulates the rights and abilities of all students to learn and to belong,

- the full school staff sharing responsibility for meeting the needs of all students in each class,

- teachers, general and special, dividing responsibilities in a collaborative design,

- teachers having time to discuss and plan ongoing instructional activities,

- support personnel being in the classroom for a long enough period of time and on a consistent enough basis for them to collaborate effectively,

- the school using natural proportions in the classroom, and home school placements for students with disabilities,

- classroom practices that recognize that students learn differently and at a varied pace,

- classroom instruction that is designed, presented, and assessed in a manner that reflects student differences,

- teachers who use educational best practices, and are sensitive to the needs of diverse learners,

- the school ensuring quality educational settings for all students,

- the school obtaining sufficient funds, allocated in a fair and equitable manner,

- the school involving parents in an effective and collaborative manner,

- ongoing assessment of the program and feedback for needed improvement.

Inclusion: A Service, Not A Place, by Dorothy Kerzner Lipsky and Alan Gartner.

BLM No. 8

QUALITY INDICATORS OF AN INCLUSIVE ENVIRONMENT

This scale can be used in a number of ways: as part of the planning process, as a school-assessment at a point in time, as a review of progress made or as a monitor of implementation.

SCHOOL CLIMATE

	Not Yet Implemented	Partially Implemented	Fully Implemented
Responsibility for ("ownership") the education of all students is shared among the entire staff.			
There is collaboration between 1) evaluators and teachers, 2) general and special education teachers, and 3) classroom personnel and other service providers.			
Collaboration between and among staff is the instructional norm and is supported by administration and other arrangements (e.g. common "prep" periods, other arrangements for joint planning, collaborators have the opportunity to spend enough time together to become partners).			
The school's administrative organization, supervisory processes, and planning bodies reflect(s) and support(s) an inclusive environment (e.g. principal sees self as responsible for the learning of all students in the building, implementation of each student's IEP, supervision and evaluation of all personnel).			
Classrooms include students with disabilities in natural proportions.			
Self-contained classrooms, if present, are distributed throughout the building with classes of grade peers.			
Special education teachers, both those who teach in regular classes and those in self-contained classes, participate in all grade activities.			

COMPREHENSIVE EDUCATION PLAN

	Not Yet Implemented	Partially Implemented	Fully Implemented
The school's planning documents and processes reflect(s) an inclusive environment (e.g. address issues of concern re: all students, including those with disabilities)			
The school leadership team reflects the full population of the school.			

BLM No. 8 (continued)

	Not Yet Implemented	Partially Implemented	Fully Implemented
CURRICULUM, INSTRUCTION & ASSESSMENT			
Regular education program is strengthened so as to enable greater numbers of students to be served in that setting (i.e., good common school).			
Student needs are met while decreasing referrals and increasing decertification, thus providing increasing percentages of students with services in the general education environment, with needed supplementary aids and services.			
Classroom activities reflect the reality that students learn differently (in manner and rate).			
All staff working in general education classrooms are provided with all instructional materials for the regular curriculum.			
Students with disabilities are enabled to, and do, participate in the full range of the school's activities, including extra-curricular activities, with needed supplementary aids and services.			
Students with disabilities participate to the fullest extent appropriate in general education classes (N.B. This involves both assuring that such participation per the student's IEP is honored and a measure of overall "inclusion," viz. IDEA's presumption that students with disabilities will be educated with their nondisabled peers, with needed supplementary aids and services.)			
Students with disabilities are included in the state- and district-wide assessment, with needed adaptations and modifications, and their results are incorporated in the school's overall reporting.			

	Not Yet Implemented	Partially Implemented	Fully Implemented
STAFF DEVELOPMENT			
The school's professional development activities address the needs of all staff (including special educators) to serve all students (including those with disabilities), so as to assure beneficial access to the general curriculum.			

BLM No. 8 (continued)

	Not Yet Implemented	Partially Implemented	Fully Implemented
SUPPORT SERVICES Support and clinical staff are effectively incorporated as integral members of the school community, in roles re: "prevention" and support services, as well as student assessment and as related services providers.			
PARENT INVOLVEMENT Parents of students with disabilities are included in all school activities (e.g., membership on the School Leadership Team and similar bodies, participation in the school's PA, involvement in other school activities).			
RESOURCES The building's resources are appropriately and equitably distributed so as to benefit all students. The resources are provided in a "placement neutral" manner, i.e. they follow the student and are not dependent on service setting.			
SCHOOL SELF-EVALUATION There is ongoing building self-evaluation to monitor progress toward goal of restructuring for quality education for all students.			

Inclusion: A Service, Not A Place, by Dorothy Kerzner Lipsky and Alan Gartner.

3
Developing a Student's Program: The Work of the IEP Team

What are the roles of the IEP Team members?
The IEP, according to the U.S. Department of Education Final Regulations on IDEA, is "the primary tool for enhancing the child's involvement and progress in the general curriculum."[5]

In the development of the IEP, federal law requires a multi-disciplinary team; actual membership is determined by state law and regulation, so long as it falls within the broad requirements of IDEA. The following must be involved on the IEP Team: the child's parent(s) or guardian(s), a person who can interpret evaluation results, special education teacher(s) or provider(s), and a representative of the school district of the student's residence. In addition, as appropriate, for the individual student,[6] regular education teacher(s) at the child's grade level (see following section for details about this), others with knowledge or special expertise about the child, and transition service agency representative(s) are also included.

The child's parent brings both the most extensive knowledge of the student and the deepest commitment to her/his development. The student represents her/his own needs and documents the reality of the process by her/his presence. The presence of varied professionals reflects the multitude of vantage points that must be considered. A representative of the school district brings to the process information about the nature of services at the various schools in the district; this person must have the authority to commit resources and be able to ensure that whatever services are set out in the IEP will actually be provided. Whenever the purpose of the meeting is to discuss a child's transition needs or services, the school must invite a representative of any other agency likely to be providing and/or paying for such services.

Without specifying the particulars of the Team's functioning, it is to be governed by team decision making, which IDEA promotes as a process built upon consensus among the members. Should consensus not be reached, there are procedures (e.g., mediation, impartial hearing, access to the courts) available both to parents and to school personnel. While the law identifies the information which must be included in the IEP, it does not specify its form or appearance. Each state may decide what its IEP will look like; in several states, individual school districts design their own IEP.

Education law requires that a program be designed to meet the student's needs, not that a student be shoe-horned into whatever program the district has available. Increasingly, there is the recognition that there are many program alternatives that can address a student's individual needs. Familiarity with these program options can enhance the quality of the IEP Team's deliberations. For parents, the opportunity to visit various program options can enhance the placement decision.

Language issues—both education jargon and for non-English speakers—often confound parental participation. The school must ensure that parental participation is not denied as a consequence of language issues. Useful here is an OSEP developed Spanish glossary with more than 200 IDEA-related terms translated from English to Spanish. Developed by a group of parents from a diversity of Spanish cultures, geographic regions, and with children of various ages and disabilities, care was taken in the development of the glossary to eliminate variances in the translation of educational terms.

What is the role of the regular education teacher in the development of the student's IEP?

IDEA requires participation on the IEP Team of one or more regular education teachers at the child's grade level, if the child is or may be participating in the general education environment. The decision about such participation belongs to the IEP Team. Many districts now routinely include a regular education teacher at such meetings.

The participation of a regular education teacher in that process brings to the table someone knowledgeable about that curriculum. At the same time, s/he can identify the supplementary aids and services needed both by the student and school staff. The federal regulations make clear the role of the regular education teacher as part of the IEP Team. "[T]he regular education teacher who is a member of the IEP Team must participate in discussions and decisions about how to modify the general curriculum in the regular classroom to ensure the child's involvement and progress in the general curriculum and participation in the regular education environment."[7] The development and proliferation of common core curriculum standards makes this participation all the more important. It also gives focus to that effort.

What are the roles of related services providers?
Related services are not ends in themselves; rather, they are activities designed to enable students to benefit from the special education services. Increasingly schools are developing related services programs that are integrated into the overall special or general education program. As students with disabilities receive a greater portion of their services in the general education classroom, related services are provided on a "push-in" basis; that is, in the regular classroom. This serves four primary functions: it offers the services in a natural rather than separate setting; it is more likely to be integrated into the regular curriculum; it reduces the amount of time that the student is removed from the regular classroom with the consequence of activities missed and the (negative) attention of moving in and out; and it provides an opportunity for general education students to receive the benefit of the services, e.g., speech, counseling, physical or occupational therapy, or specialized reading. More fundamental than the location of the service is that related services be integrated with the core curriculum.
The participation of related service providers at the IEP Team meeting is not required by law. Their participation, however, facilitates the integration of related services in the student's overall program. Related services providers must be given the completed IEP, and it is their responsibility to address the stated objectives.

How can the development of the IEP be enhanced?
When the development of the IEP is separate in time and location, rather than an integrated approach, the result may be separate activities rather than those based on the curriculum. The participation of the regular education teacher as part of the IEP Team is a step toward reducing that separation. The participation of related services providers is also valuable. Opportunities for members of the IEP Team to observe the student in classroom activities offer an additional step toward integration. Ongoing team review of student progress is essential. These do not have to be formal IEP Team meetings. When decisions are made that materially change the IEP, the meeting must be formal.

IDEA (2004) provides flexibility in the participants and development of the IEP. If the parent(s) and school district (LEA) agree, a member of the IEP team may be excused from a team meeting, the annual review may be conducted without a team meeting, and there may be alternatives to a physical meeting.

Assessing the process and product of the IEP
The IEP process, both its development and implementation, is an ongoing one. As a Team and individually[8], the following questions can serve as a guide in the IEP development and assessment.

The Content and Development Process of the IEP

Expected Outcomes

1. What are expected outcomes for children at this age/grade/educational level? Have the following been considered: academic outcomes, social/emotional outcomes, health/medical outcomes, life-skill outcomes, communication outcomes, vocational/career outcomes?
2. Are these appropriate outcomes for the student with a disability?
3. Should any of these outcomes be modified given the student's disability and its impact upon performance?
4. How should these (modified, if warranted) outcomes be reflected in the IEP goals and objectives?
5. How does the student's learning styles impact on IEP goals and objectives? In light of these, what modifications are needed in instructional methods? Curriculum? Learning environment? Instructional materials? How will these modifications be made? By whom?
6. What related and support services are necessary, in light of the goals and objectives?
7. What support and professional development needs are there for staff regarding curriculum modification? Consultation? Instructional strategies? In-class supports? Behavior?
8. How will needed planning time be provided? Who will be involved?
9. What has/has not worked in the past? In school? At home? In other settings?

Tools/Methods to Be Used to Measure Progress

1. Which of the following will be used to measure the student's academic performance: Teacher-developed testing? School/district/state standardized testing? Norm-referenced tests? Criterion-referenced tests? Review of homework/classwork? Task analyses? Mastery levels? Portfolio assessments? Performance? Parent input? Per IEP goals?
2. Which of the following will be used to measure the student's social/emotional development: Observation of on-task behavior? Observation of peer and adult/student interactions? Results of group and individual work? Self-reports? Parent reports? Per IEP goals?
3. Per these tools, is the student on track toward the established outcomes/goals? If not, are all the services being provided? Are they appropriate? Do they need to be modified/supplemented/changed? How does the student's performance compare with her/his classmates/age peers/district expectations?

Adapted from SPAN materials

Guidance for Parents
(Based on material prepared by "Kids Together," a Pennsylvania volunteer organization.) It can be useful for parents and school personnel.

<u>The IEP</u>
- The IEP should be based on a child's needs, not on what is available.
- The absence of funding, or training or staff is not an acceptable reason for not proving the needed services.
- What is being done for any other child is not the basis for your child; the IEP is about your child.
- Special education is a service, not a place. Thus, services follow the child.

<u>Prepare for meetings</u>
- Who will be attending and what is their role?
- Ask exactly what the meeting will cover.
- Agree upon an agenda.
- Make sure enough time is allotted.
- Get copies of reports and evaluations that will be discussed before the meeting.
- Prepare a vision statement for your child's future.
- Write a draft version of the IEP or at least a set of priorities.
- Bring copies of material (e.g., records of previous meeting(s), material about the child, pertinent articles).

<u>At the IEP Meeting</u>
- Never go to the meeting alone. You are entitled to invite whom you wish.
- Consider whether you think it is in the child's best interest to attend. This is your decision.
- Reschedule if the key people are not present.
- Begin the meeting with a reading of your child's vision statement.
- Have a facilitator take notes.
- Be clear and specific as to what you want. This should be about your child's needs; not broad policy discussions.
- Get the issues out in the open.
- Insist on positive language to describe your child.
- Make sure every service and support agreed upon is written in the IEP, as is who is responsible for implementing each part.
- Include a schedule of subsequent meetings in the IEP (or at least the process for setting them).
- Review the IEP before accepting it.

Where can I find additional information about the work of the IEP Team?

Bateman, Barbara D. & Cynthia M. Herr. *Writing Measurable IEP Goals and Objectives.* Verona, WI: Attainment Company, Inc., 2003.

Courtade-Little, Ginevra & Diane M. Browder. *Aligning IEPs to Academic Standards: For Students with Moderate and Severe Disabilities.* Verona, WI: Attainment Company, Inc., 2005.

Jennings, M. *Before the Special Education Referral.* Thousand Oaks, CA: Corwin Press, 2009.

McPartland, Pat. *Implementing Ongoing Transition Plans for the IEP: A Student-Driven Approach to IDEA Mandates.* Verona, WI: Attainment Company, Inc., 2005.

Moll, Anne M. *Differentiated Instruction Guide for Inclusive Teaching.* Port Chester, NY: Dude Publishing, 2003.

Schwarz, Shelley Peterman & Nancy Kruschke McKinney. *Organizing your IEPs.* Verona, WI: Attainment Company, Inc., 2005.

Siegel, Lawrence M. *Complete IEP Guide: How to Advocate for Your Special Ed Child, 2nd Edition.* Berkeley, CA: NOLO, 2001.

Twachtman-Cullen, Diane & Jennifer Twachtman-Reilly. *How Well Does Your IEP Measure Up?: Quality Indicators for Effective Service Delivery.* Higganum, CT: Starfish Specialty Press, 2002.

4
Collaboration

What is collaboration?
Collaboration is the practice that allows all staff in the school to share responsibility for meeting the needs of all students. There are a great variety of ways in which collaboration can take place. For the participants, collaboration involves a process of change from the traditional solo practice of an individual teacher and her/his class to partners working together to address the needs of all the students in the classroom. The partners share their knowledge and step out of their old roles (role release); each learns from and is dependent upon the other (interdependency). Teachers have identified that the "doing of collaboration" becomes a powerful means of professional and personal development. While some teachers may initially be reluctant to collaborate with another staff member, across the country the idea is gaining widespread acceptance.

What are the benefits of collaboration for teachers and students?
The increasing body of knowledge that students are expected to master, and the increasing diversity of America's classrooms, requires a pedagogic shift. The past model was based on one teacher providing all the needed instruction to all the students in her/his classroom. The new model is based on an education service delivery model in which two or more professionals work collaboratively to teach the material to a diverse group of learners. For the increasing number of students with disabilities served in general education classes, as well as for other students with special needs that are not identified, the collaboration of teachers with different styles, approaches, knowledge and skills allows for the teaching of the general education curricula with enhanced outcomes for all students.

The concept of teacher collaboration is in sharp contrast with the traditional consultative model, where one teacher (the consultant) is seen as more knowledgeable and the other (the consultee) is seen as in need of that expertise. In the collaborative model, two (or more) teachers have different expertise and each is expected to contribute toward the shared enterprise of providing educational opportunities for all the students.

From the perspective of the teachers, there are many benefits of collaboration. They include:

- reducing the isolation of being a solitary teacher,
- enjoying the collaboration with a colleague,
- sharing the responsibility for the teaching of a diverse group of students,
- learning new skills and approaches, and
- having a non-supervisory colleague reflect on your practice.

A range of benefits for students have been identified as a result of collaborative teaching. These include students:

- having a wider range of instructional alternatives,
- receiving less fragmented instruction (especially students with special needs),
- being less critical of others and more motivated,
- recognizing abilities among peers,
- improving academic performance,
- improving social skills,
- relating to several adults,
- developing positive peer relationships,
- seeing adults work together cooperatively,
- seeing adults disagree and work through difference(s), and
- increasing their sense of community.

> "The self-contained [special education] program assumes a ceiling on what the kids can do. With the support of two teachers in the mainstream classroom, there's no ceiling." A high school special education teacher stated, "After initial reluctance, co-teachers say they wouldn't have it any other way," (March/April, 1999) Harvard Education Letter, 15(2), p. 3.
>
> "Before we started co-teaching, I basically didn't know what my children were doing outside my room; they just went somewhere and did something. They would miss whatever was going on in my class. I wouldn't schedule a test at that time, but they missed the lesson that hour or sometimes they even missed story time, the fun part. They had to miss something. Now [with co-teaching], I'm able to expand on what they have learned." An elementary general education teacher, cited in J. E. Nowacek (1992), Professionals talk about teaching together: Interviews with five collaborating teachers, Intervention in school and clinic, 27, p. 263.]

The benefits of collaboration have been affirmed by many teachers and few choose to go back to solo practice. The culture of schools, however, often is one of isolation, where success is measured more individually than as a result of the whole team's effort. Teachers are too often cloistered behind the classroom door, and contact with colleagues, as one teacher put it, is "brief, incomplete and often inconsequential."[9] If collaboration is to succeed, it must be intentional, structured, and supported.

Professional development and opportunities to plan together are key to effective collaboration. Frequently, teacher education programs have prepared general and special education teachers in separate and isolated pre-service programs. They have provided few opportunities for future teachers to learn how to work together with a more diverse student population in restructured inclusive education classrooms.

A 2011 OSEP Project Directors conference, "How do we prepare general education and special education faculty and teachers to collaborate?" addressed these issues. Conference presenters emphasized the need for teacher education programs to reflect the inclusive reforms in classroom practice. While changes are necessary at the pre-service level, professional development opportunities must be a central aspect of a school district's efforts. This includes training in joint planning, collaboration, co-teaching, curricular adaptation, enhanced instructional strategies, classroom management, and assessment. The focus of the professional development should be on situation-specific problem solving; it should address the change process itself.

Professional development for restructured and inclusive education involves a paradigmatic shift from traditional in-service and teacher training models. In the traditional model, the teacher, either general or special education, was a qualified professional who taught in her/his own classroom. Upgrading and/or expansion of the teacher's skills was based upon the teacher's particular interest(s). In the new inclusive classroom, special and general educators come to rely upon each other's skills and knowledge, and to develop ways to work collaboratively as a team. During professional development, inclusion brings together teachers as peers, each as a "trainee" and "trainer," collaborating to become quality teachers of all students.

The process of professional development models the collaboration of the inclusive classroom and, for the students, the relationship between the two teachers models adults working together. Indeed, one of the frequent reports from successful collaborating teachers is that the students see them working together, including resolving differences in a peaceful manner.

Collaboration differs from the traditional model of the solo teacher in her/his classroom; what the late Al Shanker, past president of the American Federation of Teachers, used to call the "egg crate classroom." The collaborative model means that the services the student needs are provided by the collaborating teachers. Both are the child's teacher. As such, parents should come to know both and share with both their dreams for the child and their sense of the classroom experience.

What are the models of collaboration?

There is not one approach to collaboration. Schools often use more than one model to address the needs of their students and teachers. Among the various models in use, the six that follow are the most frequently cited:

1. ***Co-teaching, full-time:*** the most typical model. A special and general education teacher are in the same classroom, jointly sharing full responsibility for the entire class.

2. ***Co-teaching, part-time:*** a variation of the above. A special education teacher divides her/his time between multiple general education classrooms. When the special education teacher is in the classroom, the teachers will address the major academic subjects. In some districts, a paraprofessional is assigned to the class when the special education teacher is in another class.

3. ***Indirect support:*** the special education teacher provides consultative or "indirect" support to the regular education teacher in whose class students with disabilities are included.

4. ***Methods and resources:*** a special education teacher has primary responsibility for adapting materials and developing alternative instructional strategies for a number of students, often in different classrooms.

5. ***Team model:*** a special education teacher is incorporated as part of the team of general education teachers, which then serves a cohort of students, general and special education. This is a common middle school design.[10] It provides an opportunity for all of the teachers who serve students who move from class-to-class to share information about the students and the course work. At the elementary level, a special education teacher may be assigned to a grade level or work in a specific content area.

6. ***School-wide model:*** the entire staff as a group take on responsibility for all students, disabled and nondisabled, teaching in a multitude of configurations, e.g., lecturing to a large group, tutoring a small group, etc.

Suggestions for Teachers: Co-teaching Approaches

Co-teaching is the most common of the collaboration approaches. Based on their individual strengths and interests, teachers have developed many arrangements for teaching together. It is the mixture and flexibility of these arrangements that makes the collaborative process a positive experience for both teachers. The common features are: the teachers plan together; they alternate roles; and students are not divided, special and general education.

The following collaboration arrangements have been identified by teachers:

- **_Team teaching_**: both teachers deliver the same instruction at the same time.
- **_Alternative teaching:_** one teacher takes responsibility for a large group while the other works with a smaller group;
- **_Station teaching:_** teachers divide both content and students, and switch and repeat;
- **_Parallel teaching:_** both teachers are presenting the same material simultaneously, dividing the class into two groups;
- **One teach, one rotate through the classroom:** one teacher has primary responsibility for the delivery of the material, while the other circulates through the room providing assistance to the students as needed; and
- **One teach, one observe:** one teacher presents the material while the other observes the lesson and student reaction, and subsequently shares observations with his/her colleague.

Advantages and disadvantages of the various co-teaching approaches?

The collaborative models and approaches identified in the previous section each have advantages and disadvantages. They have been identified as follows (Friend, 2001).

Method	Advantages	Disadvantages
Team teaching	• Lower student-teacher ratio • Highest level of teacher collaboration	• Most complex • Most dependent upon teachers' styles of teaching
Alternative teaching	• Smaller group size • Students remain part of the community • Can use to provide enrichment, as well as support	• Can become a segregated program
Parallel teaching	• Small groups • Better student participation • Strategic grouping of students • More effective discipline	• Higher noise level • Students more easily distracted • Both teachers need to know the content • Need to cover content in similar ways • High level of trust needed between the teachers
One teach, one rotate	• Assistance regularly provided to students as needed	• One teacher put in the role of an assistant; is this the best use of professional expertise?
One teach, one observe	• More detailed observation of student learning. • Effective planning together, based on observations of student learning.	• One teacher put in the role of an assistant; is this the best use of professional expertise?

Gately and Gately (2001) emphasize interpersonal communications as key to co-teaching, identifying three stages based upon the nature of the communication:[11]

- Beginning stage: Guarded, careful communication,
- Compromising stage: Give and take communication, with a sense of having to "give" to "get,"
- Collaborating stage: Open communication and interaction, mutual admiration.[12]

They point out that at the beginning stage teachers seek to establish a professional working relationship, developing a sense of boundaries and permeabilities. For some general education teachers, there may be a sense of intrusion and invasion, while for some special education teachers there may be a sense of discomfort and exclusion. Teachers tread slowly and cautiously. Unless there is recognition of a developmental process, teachers may get "stuck" at this stage.

The compromising stage is one of give and take, with the compromises made (e.g., giving up something in order to gain something else) becoming the basis for a more collaborative process.

In the collaborative stage, there is more open communication, and a greater degree of comfort and use of humor. This is experienced not only by the teachers, but the students as well. The two teachers work together and complement each other. It has been said that students in an inclusive classroom sometimes find it difficult to discern which teacher is the special educator and which the general educator; both are teachers, no adjectives!

How does collaboration fit into IDEA and NCLB?

Collaboration is a way to address the law's presumption that students with disabilities will be served in a general education setting, with the needed supports. The law emphasizes "whole school" approaches for the education of students with disabilities. Collaboration is one of the ways that such an approach can become a reality.

The following imaginary conversation highlights the shift from separate special education services to a collaborative approach:

- "I do it all by myself," says the special education teacher of a self-contained class.
- "I do the special part myself," says the resource or "pull out" teacher or related services provider.
- "Someone else does it," says the general education teacher.
- "We do it together," says the collaborators of regular and special education.

[Adapted from DeBoer & Fister, 1994, p. 11]

While collaboration is most often considered a matter between classroom teachers, additional forms of collaboration are worth noting. These include collaboration between classroom personnel and the providers of related and resource room services. When IEP services for a student are conducted on a "pull out" basis, often they divert attention from the general education curriculum, disrupt the classroom as children move in and out, and cause students pulled out to miss important learning opportunities in the general education classroom. Increasingly, related and resource room services are being provided on a "push in"[13] basis, with these specialists infusing their services within the context of the general education curriculum and classroom.[14] A further advantage of this "push in" design is that other students, those "at risk" but not labeled as "disabled," or other general education students all can benefit from such in-class services.

Another aspect of collaboration is between those involved in student evaluation, program design and classroom personnel. The evaluation and IEP development process often is separate from the classroom activities of the student. The reauthorized IDEA requirement for the participation of a general education teacher, at the child's grade level, as a member of the IEP Team, is intended to enhance the integration of the IEP development and the classroom implementation. Additionally, opportunities for other members of the IEP Team to observe students in the classroom and to offer services within the classroom are further areas for collaboration.

The components of classroom collaboration include:
- ***Sharing responsibility:*** A change from a sense of ownership of "my" classroom to a shared responsibility, in planning and delivery for all students;
- ***Developing a shared classroom approach:*** Each will need to work with the other professional in developing classroom practices, rules, and activities;
- ***Learning collaborative skills:*** Each will need to learn the pedagogic and personal skills of collaboration, including who implements what curricula material, in which manner, for which students, and how to express disagreement;
- ***Learning from each other:*** Each must learn the assumptions, perspectives, knowledge, language, and jargon used by the partner, particularly as it relates to the other's training and expertise;
- ***Exposure:*** Each must learn to accept the close observation of her/his practice by another adult. This involves a level of exposure of one's practice, new for most teachers. Collaborative teams, over time, appreciate the sense of camaraderie.

What is the role of paraprofessionals?
Paraprofessionals have become an integral part of inclusion. This term encompasses those staff members with such titles as teacher

aide, teacher assistant, and paraeducator. When teachers have the support of a paraprofessional, collaboration is essential. Early in the implementation of P.L. 94–142, most paraprofessionals were assigned to provide assistance to individual students. In recent years, the focus has shifted to paraprofessionals working in the classroom under the guidance of the general education teacher rather than with an individual student. It is important s/he not be "velcroed" to the child with a disability, which could inhibit the student's interaction with other students in the classroom and create a dependency on the paraprofessional.

To be an effective member of the classroom's instructional team, paraprofessionals require professional development. This could include a balance between professional development exclusively with other paraprofessionals and professional development with teachers. An additional feature for paraprofessionals is the opportunity in a growing number of school districts for them to participate in a career ladder program, earning a college degree and becoming certified as a teacher. In many communities, the implementation of career ladder programs has led to positive developments: an increase in the number of teachers from the same communities as the students, teachers with a greater likelihood of staying in the school system, and teachers who begin their work as professionals with a great deal of prior experience in the schools. While the NCLB focus has been on "highly qualified teachers," the law also requires enhanced professional qualifications for paraprofessionals who work with children in instructional activities. Well developed programs of professional development, as well as careful designs of supervision (French 2008), serve to enhance the quality of services provided teachers and the paraprofessional.

What are the stages of collaboration?
In the process of implementing collaboration, four stages can be considered.

STAGE 1:
Establishing the context: Basic to collaboration is the acceptance of shared responsibility and a commitment toward all the students in the classroom. Some teachers have called this shared "ownership," or an inclusive "community of learners." There is a recognition at this stage that collaboration cannot be done without planning and discussion, sometimes including differences and disagreements.

The metaphor of a dance has been used to describe co-teaching and the process of collaboration that underlies it. "Like all dances, we must first hear the music, then learn the steps, maintain our balance, and coordinate with our partner. The actual 'messiness' of our collaborative interactions probably compares more to the 1960s rock and roll than to a stylized ballet, but the synchrony is there, nevertheless." (Halvorsen & Neary, 2001, p. 130).

STAGE 2:
Negotiating the basis of the relationship: When two teachers plan to work together in the classroom, regardless of the particular model, there are a number of questions that they should ask each other. These are called "points of negotiation" and addressing them can become the basis upon which to forge an effective partnership. There are no "right" answers to these points of negotiation. Done prior to the beginning of collaboration, they become the basis for the partners to work together. And, over time they should be revisited.

> "There were times when we disagreed, and we learned to compromise and sometimes to give the final decision to the other teacher. Our classroom management styles were also different, but we learned to find a compromise that worked for both of us. Most important, I think it was critical to inform our students of what we were doing and why. Our students understood that they would have two teachers, with equal authority and with whom they would have equal opportunities to work. Many of my students expressed that having two teachers is better because everyone gets more help." A classroom teacher in N. L. Langerock (Nov/Dec 2000), "A passion for action research," Teaching Exceptional Children, 33(2), p. 27.

The participants should consider several points in developing their collaborative approach:
- The partnership is a professional relationship, requiring respect and acceptance of shared responsibility. The metaphor of a marriage is not appropriate.
- The collaboration is an evolving relationship, not an instant arrangement.
- The roles should be structured to ensure that responsibility for all students is shared between both teachers. From the students' point of view, this means they each have two teachers.
- The strengths of each of the teachers should be maximized in determining teaching strategies to be used.
- The collaborative process should be evaluated on an ongoing basis, and in terms of student outcomes.

The **Blackline Master No. 9,** page 62, "Points of Negotiation in Collaborative Teaching," can serve as a basis for discussion between the collaborators.

STAGE 3:
Planning together: No factor is more important to the success of the collaboration than opportunity for regularly scheduled planning

time. When teachers plan together, the following should support that effort:

- regularly scheduled sessions that have a fixed start and end time;
- planned agendas;
- prior preparation and active participation of each team member;
- interruptions should be held to an absolute minimum;
- administrators should not assign teachers for another duty during planning time.

As the school's leader, the principal plays an essential role in ensuring that time for staff planning is scheduled. Schools have developed a variety of ways of accomplishing planning time. Among them are:

- common "prep" periods for the collaborating teachers;
- a "floating" substitute teacher to release the collaborating teachers;
- "per session" time, before or after school;
- compensatory time;
- part of an assigned professional activity;
- release from other duty;
- staff development days/afternoons;
- existing faculty meeting time;
- class coverage by other staff;
- incorporation within an extended instructional day;
- part of a restructured school week/year;
- administrators, deans, counselors covering a class;
- students engaged in an activity with another adult;
- enlist outside resources, including parents, community members, and college faculty; and
- dropping less essential activities.

STAGE 4:
Assessing the outcomes of collaboration: There are two sets of outcomes that warrant attention: outcomes for students, based on the standards of the curriculum, and outcomes involved in the collaboration process itself. In assessing outcomes for students, it is the school's and district's regular measures and practices that should be used, e.g., standardized tests, portfolios and performances, classroom participation, etc. The **Blackline Master No. 10,** pages 63-64, "Assessing Collaboration: A Team Study Guide," may be used as a guide to assess the process of collaboration.

The Co-teaching Rating Scales (CRS), pages 65-66, are other designs to examine the effectiveness of co-teaching classrooms.[15]

It can be used by teachers who co-teach full- or part-time. It can enable the teachers to identify areas of their collaboration that are successful, as well as to focus on areas that may need improvement. It can serve as a tool in developing co-teaching goals. There are two scales, one for the special education teacher and the other for the general education teacher. Each form asks similar questions. It is best for the teachers to complete the form independently and then to compare and discuss their answers.

What are the roles of other school personnel regarding collaboration?

To be successful, collaboration must be an essential aspect of the entire school program. Schoolwide collaboration means that all the personnel of the building work together to address the needs of all students, not only a few teachers. Administrators must convey the message in attitude and organization.

Collaboration involves a mind-set—one that recognizes that all students belong and all staff are responsible for the success of each and every student. The organization and procedures of the school are designed to express an inclusive environment; this involves a shift from a focus on "my" students to "our" students.

The necessary restructuring can best take place when collaboration is implemented as a schoolwide approach. In this, the school's administration plays an essential role. This includes the following:

- teacher schedules and student programs are developed to reflect the collaboration;
- the supervision and evaluation of collaborating teachers incorporates the realities of the collaboration; if the model of collaboration used, for a particular subject, involves one of the partners presenting the material and the other reinforcing it, the evaluation of each should take this into account.
- time is provided for the partners to plan and work together, not as a frill but as an essential part of the school's procedures;
- support and consultative services are available to the collaborators;
- a "universal design" approach is encouraged, rather than a single instructional approach that has to be modified for individual students; and
- the school recognizes diversity among students, not on a demographic basis but as expressed as differences in learning "styles," or "intelligences," or level of knowledge and skill in a particular subject area, or pace of learning.

While most often collaboration is between teachers, Villa and Thousand (2009) indicate that paraprofessionals and students can be "co-teachers." It is not the status of the individual; rather, the perspective of the team members and their shared approach to the curriculum. As schools increasingly develop virtual education programs there will be new areas for collaboration. So, too, with the rapid adoption of the "Common Core Standards."

Where can I find additional information regarding collaboration?

Carolan, J. and Giunn, A. *Differentiation: Lessons from a Master Teacher.* Educational Leadership 64 (8), 44-47.

Dieker, Lisa. *7 Effective Strategies for Secondary Inclusion* (Video). Port Chester, NY: National Professional Resources, Inc., 2006.

Dieker, L. Hines, R. *Co-Teaching in Secondary Schools: 7 Steps to Successful Inclusion* (laminated referenct guide). Port Chester, NY: Dude Publishing, 2011.

Dieker, Lisa. *Co-Teaching Lesson Plan Book.* Whitefish Bay, WI: Knowledge By Design, 2000.

Dieker, Lisa. *Demystifying Secondary Inclusion: Powerful Strategies* (DVD). Port Chester, NY: National Professional Resources, Inc., 2006.

French, N.K. *A Guide to the Supervision of Paraprofessionals* (laminated reference guide). Port Chester, NY: Dude Publishing, 2008.

Friend, M. *Co-Teach!* Greensboro, NC: Marilyn French, Inc., 2011.

Friend, Marilyn. *Complexities of Collaboration* (Video). Bloomington, IN: Forum on Education, 2000.

Friend, M. *The Co-Teaching Partnership.* Educational Leadership 64 (5), 48-51.

Friend, Marilyn. *The Power of Two: Making a Difference Through Co-Teaching, 2nd Edition* (Video). Bloomington, IN: Forum on Education, 2004.

Friend, Marilyn & Lynne Cooke. *Interactions: Collaboration Skills for School Professionals, 4th Edition.* Boston, MA: Allyn & Bacon, 2002.

Halvorsen, Ann T. & Thomas Neary. *Building Inclusive Schools: Tools and Strategies for Success.* Needham Heights, MA: 2001.

Janney, Rachel & Martha E. Snell. *Collaborative Teaming: Teachers' Guides to Inclusive Practices.* Baltimore, MD: Brookes Publishing Company, 2000.

Karten, T. *Inclusion Lesson Plan Book for the 21st Century.* Port Chester, NY: Dude Publishing, 2010.

McGregor, Gail & R. Timm Vogelsberg. *Inclusive Schooling Practices: Pedagogical and Research Foundations.* Baltimore, MD: Paul H. Brooks Publishing Co., Inc. 1998.

Sapon-Shevin, Mara. *Because We Can Change the World: A Practical Guide to Building Cooperative, Inclusive Classroom*

Communities. Boston, MA: Allyn & Bacon, 1999.

Snell, Martha E. & Rachel Janney. *Collaborative Teaming.* Baltimore, MD: Paul H. Brookes Publishing Co., Inc., 2000.

Villa, Richard A. & Jacqueline S. Thousand. *A Guide to Co-Teaching.* Thousand Oaks, CA: Corwin Press, 2004.

Villa, J. and Thousand, J. *RTI: Co-Teaching and Differentiated Instruction* (laminated reference guide). Port Chester, NY, 2011.

Villa, J., and Thousand, J., and Nevin,, A.I. *Co-Teaching at a Glance* (laminated reference guide). Port Chester, NY, 2009.

Villa, Richard A. *Collaboration for Inclusion Video Series* (Video Set). Port Chester, NY: National Professional Resources, Inc. 2002.

Villa, Richard A. & Jacqueline S. Thousand. *Restructuring for Caring and Effective Education: Piecing the Puzzle Together, 2nd Edition.* Baltimore, MD: Paul H. Brookes Publishing, 2000.

BLM No. 9

POINTS OF NEGOTIATION IN COLLABORATIVE TEACHING: A SELF-STUDY GUIDE

It is important for teams to discuss their differences and similarities. The items below have been identified as important by teachers. Complete this survey individually, and then discuss your responses with your collaborator.

Instructional methods:
What instructional methods do I generally use?
How do I learn about new instructional methods?
What additional ones would I like to use?

Instructional materials:
What instructional materials do I generally use?
How do I learn about new instructional materials?
What additional ones would I like to learn?

Assignments:
How do I currently handle student assignments? In class? As homework? What are alternative ways of handling them?

Testing and assessment:
How do I currently handle testing and assessment? What alternative ways would I like to learn?

Class rules:
What are the current class rules? What alternative can be established?

Communication:
How do I communicate with colleagues? What ways are preferred? What ways are most uncomfortable?

Division of work:
What teaching tasks do I prefer to do? Not like to do? Would I prefer rotation of roles or a fixed division of assignments?

Problem solving:
How do I handle disagreements? What is the method I use for solving problems?

Planning:
How do I currently plan to meet the curriculum objectives of each lesson? When is the best time to plan with my collaborator? Before school? After school? During school?

Parents:
What methods do I use to communicate with parents? What methods would I like to consider?

Inclusion: A Service, Not A Place, by Dorothy Kerzner Lipsky and Alan Gartner.

BLM No. 10

ASSESSING COLLABORATION: A TEAM STUDY GUIDE

It is important that partners periodically assess their collaboration. It is best to do this on an ongoing basis. After considering these issues individually, compare and discuss them with your collaborator and address any changes that should be made to strengthen your work together.

Planning:

Do we plan together? What are some examples of our planning, short- and long-range? How can we plan together better?

_____
_____
_____
_____

Interdependence:

Are we interdependent? What are some examples of our interdependence? What can we do to enhance our interdependence?

_____
_____
_____
_____

Learning from each other:

Do we learn from each other? What are some examples of our learning? How can we enhance such learning?

_____
_____
_____
_____

Satisfaction:

Am I satisfied with our collaboration? What can I do to enhance our collaboration to achieve a higher level of student outcomes? What can my collaborating partner do to achieve a higher level of student outcomes?

_____
_____
_____
_____

(continued on next page)

BLM No. 10 (continued)

Contributions:
Are each of us contributing our share? If not, what can each of us do?
_____
_____
_____
_____

Communication:
How well do we communicate? To each other? To our students? To other staff? To the parents and guardians of our students? How can we communicate more effectively to each group? How do we handle disagreements?
_____
_____
_____
_____

Reflection and evaluation of practice:
How often do we reflect upon and evaluate our teaching skills? How do we use the reflection and evaluation to improve our practice?
_____
_____
_____
_____

Support:
Do we get the needed support from each other? administration? colleagues? parents? What can we do to get more support from each group?
_____
_____
_____
_____

Parent involvement:
Are we inclusive of parental involvement? How can we achieve greater parent involvement?
_____
_____
_____
_____

Inclusion: A Service, Not A Place, by Dorothy Kerzner Lipsky and Alan Gartner.

CO-TEACHING RATING SCALE: SPECIAL EDUCATION TEACHER FORMAT

Respond to each question below by circling the number that best describes your viewpoint.

1. Rarely   2. Sometimes   3. Usually

1. I can read the nonverbal cues of my partner.	1	2	3
2. I feel comfortable moving freely about the space in the classroom.	1	2	3
3. I understand the curriculum standards in each content area.	1	2	3
4. Both teachers agree on classroom goals.	1	2	3
5. Planning can be spontaneous, with changes occurring during the instructional lesson.	1	2	3
6. I present lessons in the cotaught classroom.	1	2	3
7. Classroom rules and procedures are jointly developed.	1	2	3
8. Various measures are used for grading students.	1	2	3
9. Humor is used in the classroom.	1	2	3
10. All materials are shared in the classroom.	1	2	3
11. I know multiple methods and materials to support curriculum outcomes.	1	2	3
12. Students with disabilities are taught using the same standards as students in general.	1	2	3
13. Planning for lessons is the shared responsibility of both teachers.	1	2	3
14. The "chalk" passes freely between the two teachers, when appropriate.	1	2	3
15. A variety of classroom management techniques are used for all students.	1	2	3
16. Test modifications are commonplace, when appropriate.	1	2	3
17. Communication is effective.	1	2	3
18. Parental communication is a shared responsibility.	1	2	3
19. There is fluid positioning of teachers in the classroom.	1	2	3
19. My knowledge of the curriculum content is solid.	1	2	3
20. Student-centered objectives are incorporated into the curriculum.	1	2	3
22. Time is allotted for common planning.	1	2	3
23. Teachers are valued as equal partners in the learning process of the students.	1	2	3
24. Behavior management is a shared responsibility.	1	2	3
25. Goals and objectives in IEPs are assessed for students on an ongoing basis.	1	2	3

Adapted from Gately and Gately

CO-TEACHING RATING SCALE: GENERAL EDUCATION TEACHER FORMAT

Respond to each question below by circling the number that best describes your viewpoint.

1. Rarely   2. Sometimes   3. Usually

1. I can read the nonverbal cues of my partner.   1   2   3
2. I feel comfortable moving freely about the space in the classroom.   1   2   3
3. I understand the curriculum standards in each content area.   1   2   3
4. Both teachers agree on classroom goals.   1   2   3
5. Planning can be spontaneous, with changes occurring during the instructional lesson.   1   2   3
6. I present lessons in the cotaught classroom.   1   2   3
7. Classroom rules and procedures are jointly developed.   1   2   3
8. Various measures are used for grading students.   1   2   3
9. Humor is used in the classroom.   1   2   3
10. All materials are shared in the classroom.   1   2   3
11. I know multiple methods and materials to support curriculum outcomes.   1   2   3
12. Students with disabilities are taught using the same standards as students in general.   1   2   3
13. Planning for lessons is the shared responsibility of both teachers.   1   2   3
14. The "chalk" passes freely between the two teachers, when appropriate.   1   2   3
15. A variety of classroom management techniques are used for all students.   1   2   3
16. Test modifications are commonplace, when appropriate.   1   2   3
17. Communication is effective.   1   2   3
18. Parental communication is a shared responsibility.   1   2   3
19. There is fluid positioning of teachers in the classroom.   1   2   3
19. My knowledge of the curriculum content is solid.   1   2   3
20. Student-centered objectives are incorporated into the curriculum.   1   2   3
22. Time is allotted for common planning.   1   2   3
23. Teachers are valued as equal partners in the learning process of the students.   1   2   3
24. Behavior management is a shared responsibility.   1   2   3
25. Goals and objectives in IEPs are assessed for students on an ongoing basis.   1   2   3

Adapted from Gately and Gately

5
Supplementary Aids and Services in a Differentiated Classroom

What are supplementary aids and services? Accommodations and modifications?

Supplementary aids and services are related to instructional activities. Accommodations and modifications are related to the students' demonstration of learning outcomes. Supplemental aids and services are designed to provide supports to students with disabilities, to enable them to benefit from the educational services provided. Accommodations and modifications are designed to enable these students to demonstrate their learning. Supplementary aids and services are related to instructional activities; accommodations and modifications are related to assessment.

Supplementary aids and services are those services that a student or school staff, on the student's behalf, need to benefit from the school's offerings. As such, they can be simple or complex. They can relate to the content of the instruction (the curriculum), the process of presenting the curriculum (instructional strategies), the setting in which learning takes place (the environment). As part of the development process of the IEP, the Team must, for each student in each subject area, identify whether it is appropriate for the student to participate in the state- and district-wide assessments and, if so, whether some or all accommodations and/or modifications are appropriate. While the federal law applies only to state- and district-wide assessment, good practice warrants the use of the same adaptations in classroom and school assessment activities.

When the learning consequence of the student's disability requires that a supplementary aid or service be provided for instruction, it is likely that a parallel accommodation or modification will be required in assessing the student's learning. For example, a student who requires instruction using Braille material will in all likelihood require Braille material for assessment. A student who needs extra time or material on tape to master the curriculum will probably require extra time or material on tape to demonstrate her/his knowledge on the assessment.

In the 1997 IDEA amendments, as well as in IDEA (2004) and in NCLB, the Congress expressed the expectation that the great bulk of students with disabilities would participate in these assessments. When this is not to be the case, the IEP Team must describe how the student's learning will be assessed, i.e., an alternate assessment. The differences between accommodations, modifications, and alternate assessment are discussed on the pages that follow.

Historically, as students with disabilities have come to be served in general education classrooms, teachers have "retrofitted" the curriculum and adapted their instructional practices. Such adaptations would be specified on a student's IEP. Rather than a focus on the adaptations solely to address the needs of a student with a disability, a proactive approach has developed, designed to make the curriculum accessible to a diverse group of students.

> The task becomes one of integrating knowledge about curriculum and new curriculum trends with expectations about how learners with diverse characteristics will interact with the content. Through such collaborative discussions—and, then, actions—teachers can shape what goes on in the classroom to the advantage of all students before presenting content, rather than after a student encounters difficulty.[16]

The term "universal design" has been used to describe this "front-loading" or proactive approach. As a result, there is likely to be less need to provide specific adaptations for a student in a differentiated classroom, as that classroom has flexibility built in.

Universal design has come to play a growing role as part of overall approaches to teaching, learning, and assessment. Developed by the Center for Applied Special Technology (CAST), the underlying principle is that curriculum should be "universally designed" to accommodate diverse learners, in the same way that universally designed buildings are designed to accommodate people with diverse physical abilities. In the universally designed classroom, teachers present material in diverse ways (not just "chalk and talk"), students use alternative means for note-taking, and demonstrate what they know (and can do) in multiple ways. Several states (and districts) now provide training to school personnel in the application of universal design to curriculum development, technology planning, and classroom practices. There is growing recognition of the value universal design can have for inclusive education. As part of its mandate for participation of students with disabilities in state and district-wide tests, IDEA (2004) requires to the extent feasible adherence to universal design principles.[17] (See Chapter 8, Technology, including Universal Design for Learning, for more information on this topic.)

How do supplementary aids and services, and accommodations and modifications, relate to the law?

Providing individualized assistance to students has long been a hallmark of special education programs, addressed since 1975 in the regulations derived from the federal law. In the 1997 reauthorized IDEA, the Congress increased the salience of supplementary aids and services by including them in the law itself. As part of each student's IEP, the IEP Team now must consider the needed supplementary aids and services, as well as needed accommodations and modifications in state- and district-wide assessments. These provisions are maintained in IDEA (2004).

The provision of needed supplementary aids and services to students with disabilities served in general education classes marks the difference between "dumping" and the provision of the student's entitlement to an appropriate education in the least restrictive environment. The keys to the development of appropriate supplementary aids and services for students with disabilities served in the general education environment are the provisions of the reauthorized IDEA. They include:

- general education teachers, at the student's grade level, are to be a part of the team that develops each student's IEP, if the child is, or may be, participating in general education classes.
- the general education teacher, as a member of the IEP Team, is to participate in the development of the IEP, including determination of needed program modifications, supplementary aids and services as support for the student and school personnel. The general education teacher must also participate in the review and revision of the IEP and ensure the necessary supports for the student and the teacher so as to enable the child to succeed in the general education classroom.
- enhanced federal support is available for professional development, including that of general education personnel who serve students with disabilities.

In developing the IEP, the Team must consider the student's strengths, parental concerns, and the results of the most recent evaluation. To address the unique needs of each student, the IEP Team must consider:

- behavioral interventions, i.e., strategies including positive behavioral interventions and supports to address behaviors that impede learning;[18]
- language needs, i.e., in the case of a student who is limited English proficient, the IEP Team must consider the language needs of the student;

- communication needs, i.e., in the case of a student who is deaf or hard of hearing, the IEP Team must consider the language and communication needs of the student;
- instruction in Braille, i.e., in the case of a child who is blind or visually impaired, the prescribed program must provide instruction in Braille and the use of Braille, unless the IEP Team determines that instruction in Braille or the use of Braille is not appropriate; and
- assistive technology devices and services.[19]

What are differentiated classrooms and the "best practices" for them?

A differentiated classroom can serve all the students in a school. The focal point of the classroom is the students, not the curriculum. It builds on the premise that students are different in their readiness, interests, and needs in each curriculum area. In the differentiated classroom, the teacher varies the material, the instructional approach, and the manner in which the students demonstrate their learning.

The Differentiated Classroom

A differentiated classroom incorporates many of the current educational reform ideas. These include:

- students and teachers work to be respectful of each other by accepting and appreciating one another's similarities and differences;
- teachers gather information about student readiness, interests, and learning style(s) on a continuing basis;
- teachers use student information to provide varied learning options and concepts;
- students have interesting, important, and powerful learning experiences;
- students use essential skills to complete open-ended problems related to key concepts and principles;
- teachers present lessons at different levels to ensure challenges for all students;
- teachers offer students learning choices related to topics, learning styles, communication and classroom;
- information is presented to students in varied ways, including orally, visually, demonstration, part to whole, and whole to part;
- varied instructional approaches are used to address individual student needs;
- students collaborate with peers and teachers;
- teachers serve as "coaches," attending to individual students and the whole class;

- teachers support student learning along a continuum of growth, with no ceiling;
- groups are varied according to need to ensure against tracking;
- teachers design homework to extend the learning of all students;
- multiple assessment options are used to determine student learning on a continuous basis;
- reporting to parents is continuous, based on individual growth.[20]

Many of the concepts of a differentiated classroom have proven effective in earlier educational innovations, e.g., the Adaptive Learning Environment Model (ALEM), developed in the 1980's by Margaret Wang. A differentiated classroom is supported by Gardner's formulation that students have "multiple intelligences," and "jagged profiles," having greater or less strengths in some intelligences. More about the intelligences can be found on pages 84-85.

A number of factors have been identified in a differentiated classroom. In particular, the teacher makes an ongoing effort at differentiating what is taught, how the teaching approach responds to student differences, and why particular materials are used or modified to enhance learning. The basic features of a differentiated classroom include variations in three areas: instructional strategies, organiza-tional strategies, and environmental supports.

Instructional strategies that support a differentiated classroom:
- stations: different locations in the classroom where groups or individual students can work on various tasks simultaneously and then progress to another station;
- centers: physical locations in the classroom for distinct topical areas (e.g., science, art, writing, etc.);
- cooperative learning: students work in small groups with members at different levels of expertise;[21]
- multiple intelligences: offers varying entry points into a subject (e.g., narration, logical/quantitative, aesthetic, musical, experiential, environmental), as well as ways to pursue content and demonstrate outcomes;
- multi-level instruction: maintains a common focus on essential learning/skills, while enabling a tiering of experiences and out-comes; (the teacher identifies the learning expected of all students, of most students, and of a few students, and addresses all three groups in the lesson);
- learning contracts: a student works independently, while main-taining teacher direction of what is to be learned; and
- universal design: a variety of formats are used in presenting curricula, in terms of physical access to the material (e.g., text, speech, large print, Braille, graphically), learning access (e.g.,

material at various reading levels[22]), and cognitive access (e.g., embedding prompts and questions in the text that encourage reciprocal teaching).

Organizational strategies that support a differentiated classroom:

Directions:
- start the class with a familiar activity, and then meet with small groups as to their specific activity;
- alert the group to tomorrow's tasks; use task cards that identify the task at a work station or center;
- tape-record instructions; put directions on a flip chart or chalkboard.

Student-teacher signaling systems:
- students use a sign or flagging system on their desk to let the teacher know they have completed the work or need help;
- students write their names on the chalkboard;
- students take a number;
- teacher signals to control noise levels.

Organization:
- establish positive behavior rules and consequences for positive or negative behavior;
- organize/code places for student work; provide student work folders;
- listing skills and competencies for various activities;
- expand the skills and competencies to various levels;
- take notes as you rotate around the classroom;
- establish start-up and closing procedures for activities.

Physical environment supports of a differentiated classroom:
- utilize floor space particularly for students with physical mobility needs;
- arrange furniture to encourage students working together;
- make equipment and computers available for all students, with adequate storage space for student work.

What are supplementary aids and services "best practices"?

Supplementary aids and services are the instructional supports needed by students and their teacher(s) to enable the student to succeed in the general education environment. These can include:
- adaptations in the physical environment;
- adaptations in tasks assigned and materials provided;

- curricular adaptations and modifications;
- alternative instructional strategies;
- use of additional personnel (e.g., paraprofessionals and classroom aides);
- consultation between the classroom teacher(s) and other school/agency personnel;[23]
- behavior intervention plans;
- use of assistive technology.

Supplementary aids and services can be organized in multiple ways. One way is to think along the following four dimensions: the physical dimension, the instructional dimension, the social/behavioral dimension, and the collaborative dimension.[24]

The chart on page 86, "Supplementary Aids and Services: Four Dimensions," expands on these. The guide may be used by the IEP Team or other professional staff, e.g. teachers, related services providers, etc.

The **Blackline Master No. 11,** pages 87–89, "is a comprehensive listing of teacher-developed materials related to supplementary aids and services.

As part of its comprehensive redesign of special education services, and in an effort to provide inclusive opportunities for students with disabilities, the San Francisco Unified School District correlated some twenty common instructional strategies and modifications with the content standard areas the district has adopted and student learning styles. See pages 90–96.

A conceptual scheme developed at the Center for School and Community Integration identifies nine types of SAS adaptations.[25]

Size: Adapt the number of items that the learner is expected to learn or complete. For example, fewer comprehension questions for the student to complete.

Difficulty: Adapt the skill level or problem type. For example, ask questions that require only factual answers.

Input: Adapt the way instruction is delivered to the learner. For example, read the questions and discuss them before having students respond.

Output: Adapt how the student can respond to instruction. For example, permit the student to draw a picture or write a sentence that shows story comprehension.

Support: Increase the amount of personal assistance provided to the learner. For example, pair students and allow them to take turns answering.

Time: Adapt the time allotted and allowed for learning task completion, or testing. For example, provide the material to the student prior to the assignment being due or the test scheduled.

Degree of participation: Adapt the extent to which the learner is actively involved in the task. For example, involve the student in listening to the group discussion but do not require written comprehension questions.

Alternate goals: Adapt the goals or outcome expectations while using the same materials. For example, change the goal to listening for enjoyment; do not require comprehension questions.

Substitute curriculum: Provide different instruction and materials to meet a student's individual goals. For example, have the student find the date and time of favorite TV shows using the newspaper or TV Guide.

A three-step "hands-on" approach to addressing the curriculum challenge was developed by Dr. Anne M. Moll at Bellarmine College in Kentucky. The information below is adapted from her work.

STEP 1: Know Your Students
The more the teacher knows each student's interests, needs, and abilities, the better the match between curriculum, assessment and instruction, and actual learning. The following questions can serve as a guide in designing and implementing instruction.

- What are the interests of the student?
- What aspects of the language of instruction does the student understand?
- What aspects of the student's adaptive behavior impact learning?
- What physical issues does the student have that might impact learning?
- What curriculum knowledge does the student know?
- What sensory-motor skills does the student have that might impact learning?
- What assessment methods can best demonstrate student knowledge?
- What learning strategies does the student use?

STEP 2: Determine the curriculum/content
Check your state, district, and school curriculum requirements and national standards for the field. Do not depend upon textbooks alone, unless the district has already aligned them with the state/national standards. No single text will meet the needs of all students. The following questions can serve as a guide in developing curriculum and content.

- What is the expected curriculum for this age/grade level? At the local/national levels?
- How are these expectations assessed?
- What are the expectations of previous knowledge in each curricular area?
- What skills are required?
- How were students prepared for this curricular level?
- What is the language used in the instruction?
- What problem solving skills are needed?
- What socialization skills are required?
- What knowledge does a student need?[26]

  Need to know: The knowledge that is most basic and extremely important to the next level of curriculum learning. Critical concepts or skills all students are expected to gain. Essential knowledge.

  Nice to know: The knowledge that is good to know and adds depth of the student's understanding of the concept or skill, but is not necessarily the most critical information. Important knowledge.

  Excellent to know: The greater the depth of the content or skill, the more learning is enhanced. This knowledge is not expected to be mastered by all students. Good knowledge.

The levels of knowledge for a health unit are illustrated below.

Content	Need	Nice	Excellent
Need food to live	X		
Water is essential	X		
Basic food groups	X		
Eat for a variety of reasons	X		
Fats are energy	X		
Carbohydrates, proteins, & fats provide energy	X		
Vitamins & Minerals keep the body working		X	
Two types of vitamins		X	
Three types of carbohydrates		X	
Nine amino acids			X

STEP 3: Developing an instructional plan

Using the material developed regarding prior student knowledge and the curricular content, a teacher can develop an instructional plan that takes into consideration the classroom and the "real world." The following questions can serve as a guide in developing the instructional plan.

Guiding questions:
- When and where will students use the curriculum in the "real world"?
- Why is the information important for them to know?
- What contexts are appropriate for the student to use this information?
- What methods are to be used to assess student knowledge?
- How will the student demonstrate knowledge in the "real world"?

Three broad principles identified by school districts implementing inclusive education programs can guide planning for supplementary aids and services. NCERI reports they are:

1. Supplementary aids and services, while designed to address the needs of a particular child with a disability, provide benefit for all students, i.e., the classroom becomes a more effective environment for the learning of all.
2. Instructional strategies used in inclusive classrooms are practices recommended by educational researchers for students in general. As teachers report, "Good teaching is good teaching is good teaching."
3. In considering supplementary aids and services, they should be "only as special as necessary."[27]

This last point warrants amplification. In initial efforts to provide integrated opportunities for students with disabilities, there was a tendency to provide maximal supports. The excess of support, in many cases, became disabling rather than enabling. Adaptations are undesirable if they single out the student with a disability, over-emphasize the student's differences, and/or separate the student with disability from other students in the classroom. The practice of assigning an aide or paraprofessional to an individual student with disabilities, rather than to the whole classroom, may result in the student with disability becoming the responsibility of the aide rather than the teacher(s). In effect, a zealous aide may become "velcroed" to the student with disability.

In providing any type of support, it is essential to consider the preferences and reactions of the students themselves, particularly including the age- and cultural-appropriateness of the intervention. A study of social supports points to the gap between those strategies preferred by students and those used by teachers. The teachers leaned toward solving problems for the students rather than involving the students in the problem-solving. Teachers were more likely to focus on strategies that dealt with problem behaviors, conflict situations, and social and academic difficulties in the classroom, rather than using preventive strategies to foster social support, such as promoting respect, acceptance and belonging where relationship-building and cooperative activities are encouraged.[28] Given the finding that as students with disabilities become older, their willingness and confidence in their ability to self-advocate declines, it is important that students at all grade levels are provided with opportunities to take responsibility for their own learning, and to learn the skills necessary to advocate for themselves and to address their own needs.

The phrase "natural supports" is used to describe those activities and resources present or available for the inclusion of students with disabilities in the classroom. They are not so special as to mitigate against membership in the class community.

Natural supports: Resources for an inclusive classroom[29]

Staff members:
- flexibility in role activities
- role release
- teaming and sharing
- role clarification that encourages collaboration
- use of classroom aides/paraprofessionals for class, not exclusively for student(s) with disabilities

Curriculum and instruction:
- cooperative learning activities
- infusion of disability-related topics as a regular part of the curriculum
- modifications that are less obvious and stand out less
- activities that benefit disabled and nondisabled students

Space:
- (re)arrange space to benefit those with attention difficulties
- a cooling-off area/system, available to all students
- random (and varied) assignment of students, disabled and nondisabled
- opportunities for students to move about/leave the classroom

Peers:
- student assistance program available to all students
- peer tutoring, making the classroom less teacher-centric
- peer tutoring that rotates and enables students to be both tutor and tutee
- cooperative learning activities
- activities that promote social networking

Developing an Instructional Unit

A starting point for teachers in developing an instructional unit is the unit planning pyramid.[30] It allows the teacher to distinguish, for each subject area unit, what all students should learn, what most students should learn, and what some students should learn. The first category (the base of the pyramid) includes the most important concepts and is conceptually broader. The next category (the middle of the pyramid) represents the material of next greatest importance, e.g., additional facts, extension of base concepts, related concepts, more complex concepts. The last level (the top of the pyramid) may be considered supplemental material, more complex and/or more detailed. In thinking about each level, the teacher needs to consider the materials and resources needed, instructional strategies and adaptations, and evaluation and product outcomes. Given Gardner's concept of "jagged profiles" among students, i.e., stronger in some intelligences, as well as IDEA's requirement to recognize student differences subject-area-by-subject-area, individual students may be in different segments of the pyramid for different subject areas.

In developing a program for an individual student with educational needs, a teacher can consider a continuum of adaptations, from the least to the most significant.[31]

> *Least significant adaptations:* content remains the same; presentation and assessment may be slightly altered; examples include use of many visuals, preview-review lessons, use of cooperative groups, use of large print materials, use of peer coaching, giving students more time to complete tasks, use of amplification systems, student dictates responses to test/quiz questions, use of performance-based assessment.
>
> *Moderately significant adaptations:* standards stay the same or are slightly altered; more significant adaptations are made in pre-senting the lesson and in assessment; examples include use of taped lessons, changed sequence, smaller units, altered pace of instruction, off-level testing, reduced number and/or complexity of items, use of performance-based assessment.
>
> *Most significant adaptations:* major changes in standards; an expanded curriculum may be needed to include career/vocational and functional life skills: in some cases, an alternative curriculum is necessary; instructional techniques and assessment may involve use of assistive technology; examples include drawings to represent concepts, matching visual symbols with concepts, role playing, teacher observation, inventories, and use of communication boards.

While each student's program must be individual, and specified in her/his IEP, in broad terms one can expect that the great majority of students with disabilities will only need the least significant adaptations.

In considering adaptations, teachers can use the questions below:
- How much additional time and resources are required?
- What strategies will be most effective?
- Will the classroom environment require significant changes?
- Are the adaptations consistent with the teacher's philosophical orientation?
- Are they age-appropriate, unobtrusive, and perceived as fair?
- Will the adaptation support or have a negative consequence for other students in the classroom?[32]

Extracurricular activities: Based on IDEA and federal legislation, a school district has an obligation to provide curricular services to students with disabilities and to afford them the opportunity to participate in school-conducted or sponsored extracurricular activities. As in the academic area, participation of a student with disability may not be denied solely based upon the disability. The provision of supplementary aids and services is required; however, the activity must not be changed so extensively as to lose its integrity. According to law, there are many distinctions that schools need to consider. While there is no obligation for a school to waive competitive standards and allow a student with disability who does not meet the standards to participate on the varsity basketball team, participation by a student with disabilities in an after-school intramural may be required by law.

What are accommodations and modifications "best practices" in assessment?

Accommodations and modifications in assessments are not intended to give the student with disability an unfair advantage. Rather, they are required by law to enable students with a disability to demonstrate their knowledge, without being impeded by their disability.

IDEA distinguishes among accommodations, modifications, and an alternate assessment. "Accommodations" is used to define changes in format, response, setting, timing or scheduling and do not alter, in a significant way, the test measurement or the comparability of scores. In contrast, when the assessment alters the test measurement or the comparability of scores, the term "modifications" is used. "Alternate assessment" is understood to mean an assessment for students with disabilities who are unable to participate in general large-scale assessments used by a state or district, even when accommodations or modifications are used.[33] These features of IDEA are expanded and reinforced by NCLB.

The principles below are a guide to determine accommodations for students with disabilities:

- accommodations or modifications are needed by some students.
- accommodations or modifications should be determined specific to each subject area.
- the IEP Team has the authority to determine the needed accommodation or modification. Some states[34] (and districts) have lists of officially approved accommodations and should be consulted as part of IEP Team's determination.
- accommodations or modifications should be integrated into classroom instruction.
- accommodations or modification must not compromise the intent of the assessment.
- only those accommodations or modifications that are needed should be used.

The requirement that students with disabilities participate in district- and state-wide assessments is in keeping with the mandates of IDEA and NCLB. Whether their participation involves the use of accommodations, modifications, or alternate assessments, the scores of students with disabilities are to be aggregated with the scores of all other students, as well as disaggregated. The aggregated scores emphasize the "whole school" approach to the education of students with disabilities, making their outcomes a part of the school's results. The disaggregated scores allow for identifying more specific outcomes for students with disabilities, precluding their being masked in an overall average. This disaggregation is a key requirement of NCLB, reinforcing the provisions of IDEA.

Accommodations and modifications may be grouped into the following categories:

Timing: changes in duration
- extended time
- frequent breaks

Scheduling: changes in time of testing
- over several days
- at a particular time of the day
- changed order to sub-tests

Setting: changes in the location
- preferential seating (i.e., a particular place in the classroom)
- separate location
- specialized setting (i.e., with noise buffers, special lighting, etc.)

Presentation: changes in material used
- Braille, large print, large answer bubbles, fewer items per page
- read test and/or directions
- reread instructions
- cues (e.g., highlighting key words or phrases, symbol cues)
- prompts
- clarification (e.g., explain the directions, provide extra examples)
- templates (e.g., mask part of the page, yet to be addressed or already completed)
- markers (i.e., assist student in identifying place in text)
- magnifying and/or amplification devices

Response: changes in demonstration of knowledge
- student marking in test booklet (instead of on answer form)
- use of a scribe to record answers
- fewer choices in a multiple choice test
- provide examples prior to formal testing
- verbal response
- special paper (i.e., allows aligning responses)
- math tools (e.g., number lines, arithmetic tables, manipulatives, calculators)
- reference materials (e.g., dictionaries, vocabulary bank, spell checkers)
- technology (respond on a computer)
- point to answer

The "Inclusion Accommodations Chart," on pages 97-99, provides an outstanding summary of ways in which students with disabilities can be accommodated through a variety of carefully designed strategies.

Grading

While the reauthorized IDEA and NCLB specifically address participation of students with disabilities in state- and district-wide assessment programs, they do not address the matter of student grading. In the absence of direction from the federal law, decisions as to grading need to be made in the context of state and district policies. Tomlinson makes the cogent point that grading practices should grow from a philosophy of teaching and learning that respects student differences and reflects individual growth.[35] Looking at grading from her perspective as a teacher, she proposes the following:

- student's success must reflect the degree of his/her own growth;
- the grade for a student's work should be on the basis of clearly delineated criteria for the particular work assignment;

- grading should provide consistent and meaningful feedback to the student, in a way that clarifies present successes and next learning steps;
- report grades should reflect growth patterns;
- on report cards, parents should be able to see both individual student growth and relative standing.[36]

IDEA and NCLB emphasize mastery of the regular curriculum and a presumption that services for students with a disability are provided in the general education environment. Students with disabilities served in the general education classroom should be graded in a manner consistent with their nondisabled peers, when appropriate. As schools have increased inclusive practices, many alternative grading approaches have been developed to be used for all students. They can be used by teachers in a classroom alone or by those who collaborate with another teacher(s). Salend describes a number of different alter-native grading schemes.

Grading Schemes

IEP grading: Grade is determined in the context of the student meeting her/his IEP goals.

Student self-comparison: Based upon teacher and student agreement as to goals, grade is determined based upon progress toward meeting them.

Contract grading: There is an agreed upon "contract" between teacher(s) and student, that specifies outcomes, products to demonstrate mastery, evaluation strategies, and time lines.

Pass/fail: Mastery of material receives a "pass" grade.

Mastery level/criterion systems: Per particular learning activities, mastery levels are determined and their achievement measured.

Checklists: Similar to mastery standards.

Multiple grading: Grades for different factors, such as ability, achieve-ment, and effort are used.

Level grading: A subscript denotes the level of difficulty upon which the grade was based.

Descriptive grading: Teachers provide descriptive comments assessing student achievement.[37]

Where can I find additional information regarding differentiated classrooms, supplementary aids and services, accommodations and modifications?

The concept of a differentiated or student-focused classroom builds upon the work of many practitioners, researchers, and theoreticians noted below. Also, supplementary aids and services and accommodations or modifications are addressed in these sources.

Bender, William. *Differentiating Instruction for Students with Learning Disabilities.* Thousand Oaks, CA: Corwin Press, 2002.

Casbarro, Joseph. *Test Anxiety & What You Can Do About It: A Practical Guide for Teachers, Parents, & Kids.* Port Chester, NY: Dude Publishing, 2005.

Deiner, Penny Low. *Resources for Educating Children with Diverse Abilities, 4th Edition.* Florence, KY: Thomson Delmar Learning, 2004.

Gregory, Gale and Carolyn Chapman. *Differentiated Instructional Strategies: One Size Doesn't Fit All.* Thousand Oaks, CA: Corwin Press, 2002.

Heacox, Diane. Differentiated Instruction: *How to Reach and Teach All Learners (Grades 3–12).* Minneapolis, MN: Free Spirit Press, 2002.

Iervolino, Constance & Helene Hanson. *Differentiated Instructional Practice Video Series: A Focus on Inclusion (Tape 1), A Focus on the Gifted (Tape 2).* Port Chester, NY: National Professional Resources, Inc. 2003.

Janney, Rachel & Martha E. Snell. *Modifying Schoolwork: Teachers' Guides to Inclusive Practices, 2nd Edition.* Baltimore, MD: Paul H. Brookes Publishing Co., Inc., 2004.

Jensen, Eric. *Different Brains, Different Learners: How to Reach the Hard to Reach.* San Diego, CA: The Brain Store, 2000.

Jensen, Eric. *Practical Applications of Brain-Based Learning.* Port Chester, NY: National Professional Resources, Inc., 2000.

Karten, T. *Inclusion strategies that work: Research-based methods for the classroom.* Thousand Oaks, CA: Corwin Press, 2010.

Karten, T. *Inclusion succeeds with effective strategies: Grades K-5* (laminated reference guide). Port Chester, New York: Dude Publishing, 2009.

Kleinert, Harold L. & Jacqui F. Kearns. *Alternate assessment: Measuring Outcomes and Supports for Students with Disabilities.* Baltimore, MD: Brookes Publishing Company, Inc., 2001.

Moll, Anne M. *Differentiated Instruction Guide for Inclusive Teaching.* Port Chester, NY: Dude Publishing, 2003.

Munk, Dennis D. *Solving the Grading Puzzle for Students with Disabilities.* Whitefish Bay, WI: Knowledge by Design, Inc., 2003.

Rief, Sandra F. *ADHD & LD: Powerful Teaching Strategies & Accommodations* (Video). Port Chester, NY: National Professional Resources, Inc., 2004.

Teele, Sue. *Rainbows of Intelligence: Raising Student Performance Through Multiple Intelligences* (Video). Port Chester, NY: National Professional Resources, Inc., 2000.

Thomlinson, Carol Ann. *How to Differentiate Instruction in Mixed-Ability Classrooms, 2nd Edition.* Alexandria, VA: ASCD, 2001.

THE MULTIPLE INTELLIGENCES TABLE

INTELLIGENCE	WHAT IS IT?	STUDENTS LIKE TO	TEACHERS CAN
Interpersonal	• Sensitive to the feelings and moods of others. • Understands and interacts effectively with others.	• Enjoy many friends. • Lead, share, mediate. • Build consensus and empathize with others. • Work as an effective team member.	• Use cooperative learning. • Assign group projects. • Give students opportunities for peer teaching. • Brainstorm solutions to problems. • Create situations in which students are given feedback from others.
Intrapersonal	• Sensitive to one's own feelings and moods. • Knows own strengths and weaknesses. • Uses self-knowledge to guide decision-making and set goals.	• Control own feelings and moods. • Pursue personal interests and set individual agendas. • Learn through observing and listening. • Use metacognigive skills.	• Allow students to work at own pace. • Assign individual, self-directed projects. • Help students set goals. • Provide opportunities for students to get feedback from each other. • Involve the students in journal writing and other forms of reflection.
Bodily-Kinesthetic	• Uses one's body to communicate and solve problems. • Is adept with objects and activities involving fine or gross motor skills.	• Play sports and be physically active. • Use body language. • Do crafts and mechanical projects. • Dance, act or mime.	• Provide tactile and movement activities. • Offer role playing and acting opportunities. • Involve the students in physical activity. • Allow the students to move while working.
Linguistic	• Thinks in words. • Uses language and words in many different forms to express complex meanings	• Tell jokes, riddles or puns. • Read, write or tell stories. • Use an expanded vocabulary. • Play word games. • Create poems and stories using the sounds and imagery of words.	• Use sewing, model-making and other activities using fine motor skills. • Create reading and writing projects. • Help the students prepare speeches. • Interest the students in debates. • Make word games, crossword puzzles and word searches. • Encourage the use of puns, palindromes and outrageous words.

Created by faculty of the New City School, 1996, and found in *Succeeding with Multiple Intelligences: Teaching Through the Personal Intelligences;* editors Sally Boggeman, Tom Hoerr, and Christine Wallach. www.newcityschool.org

THE MULTIPLE INTELLIGENCES TABLE (continued)

INTELLIGENCE	WHAT IS IT?	STUDENTS LIKE TO	TEACHERS CAN
Logical-Mathematical	• Approaches problems logically. • Understands number and abstract patterns. • Recognizes and solves problems using reasoning skills.	• Work with numbers, figure things out and analyze situations. • Know how things work. • Ask questions. • Exhibit precision in problem solving. • Work in situations in which there are clear black and white solutions.	• Construct Venn diagrams. • Use games of strategy. • Have students demonstrate understanding using concrete objects. • Record information on graphs. • Establish time lines and draw maps.
Musical	• Sensitive to non-verbal sounds in the environment, including melody and tone. • Aware of patterns in rhythm, pitch and timbre.	• Listen to and play music. • Match feelings to music and rhythms. • Sing, hum and move to music. • Remember and work with different musical forms. • Create and replicate tunes.	• Rewrite song lyrics to teach a concept. • Encourage students to add music to plays. • Create musical mnemonics. • Teach history through music of the period. • Have students learn music and folk dancing from other countries.
Naturalist	• Sensitive to the natural world. • Sees connections and patterns within the plant and animal kingdoms.	• Spend time outdoors. • Observe plants, collect rocks and try to catch animals. • Listen to the sounds created in the natural world. • Notice relationships in nature. Categorize and classify flora and fauna.	• Use the outdoors as a classroom. • Have plants and animals in the classroom for which students are responsible. • Conduct hands-on science experiments. • Create a nature area on the playground.
Spatial	• Perceives the visual world accurately. • Creates mental images. • Thinks three-dimensionally. • Aware of relationship between objects in space.	• Doodle, paint, draw or create three-dimensional representations. • Look at maps. • Work puzzles or complete mazes. • Take things apart and put them back together.	• Draw maps and mazes. • Lead visualization activities. • Provide opportunities to show understanding through drawing or painting. • Have students design clothing, buildings, play areas and scenery.

Created by faculty of the New City School, 1996, and found in *Succeeding with Multiple Intelligences: Teaching Through the Personal Intelligences;* editors Sally Boggeman, Tom Hoerr, and Christine Wallach. www.newcityschool.org

SUPPLEMENTARY AIDS AND SERVICES: FOUR DIMENSIONS.

Below is a list of suggestions related to four dimensions of supplementary aids and services.

1. *Physical dimension:*
   - Could the classroom be made more accessible for the student?
   - Could a different size/shape table be available for small group work?
   - Does the student need to be specially positioned?
   - _____

2. *Instructional dimension:*
   - Does the student need visual aids, large print, alternative media?
   - Could the student be provided reading guides or tape-recorded texts?
   - Could the student be allowed extra time for completion of assignments, have shortened assignments, be provided with a calculator or word processor?
   - Could the student have take home or oral tests? Could the student use a study guide during tests? Could tests be shortened? Divided in parts to be taken over an extended period of time?
   - Could the student be graded pass/fail? Or receive IEP progress grading?
   - Could cooperative learning or reciprocal teaching be used? Could a partner be assigned?
   - Could the student work on related activities?
   - Could the student work on alternative skills?
   - Could the student be provided computer-assisted instruction, communication switches or software? Does the student require electronic aids or services?
   - _____

3. *Social/behavioral dimension:*
   - Could the student be involved in social skill instruction?
   - Does the student need counseling?
   - Does the student need a behavior management plan?
   - Could the student use -self--monitoring of target behaviors?
   - Could peers be used to monitor and/or redirect behavior? Could peers provide instructional assistance?
   - Could group support activities be initiated?
   - _____

4. *Collaborative dimension:*
   - Does the student require assistance from a paraprofessional or aide? On an individual basis? For what activities?
   - Does the student need additional strategy or study skill training?
   - Could the teacher(s) receive assistance from a curriculum consultant, instructional specialists, behavior specialist?
   - Could the student be served in a classroom staffed by a regular and special educator? If so, how would this be organized? How will the teachers plan and work together?
   - _____

BLM No. 11

SUPPLEMENTARY AIDS & SERVICES: TEACHER DEVELOPED EXAMPLES

The following are examples of supplementary aids and services that support student learning. They have been compiled from teacher responses.

Modify the environment:
- seat students in the classroom according to needs (e.g., attention, hearing, vision, behaviors),
- assign seats to students with audiology deficits away from noise,
- reduce visual distractions,
- ensure adequate ventilation,
- limit oral distractions (i.e., noise),
- consider using workspace other than student's desk,
- establish a daily routine, and post the daily schedule,
- clear student's work area of unnecessary/distracting material.

Modify the pace:
- reduce or substitute assignments,
- minimize recopying tasks,
- minimize copying tasks when a word or phrase will do,
- allow breaks and transition time,
- vary activities,
- allow additional time to preview materials, complete tasks, review material,
- use a timer to indicate pace.

Modify the materials used in the classroom:
- fold or line paper for spatial or organizational support,
- utilize different types of paper,
- use a whiteboard for easier vision,
- reduce excess materials on desk,
- use grip on pen/pencil,
- use highlighting or color coding for directions, key words, topic sentences, summary, etc.,
- tape record directions/assignments,
- read written questions/directions aloud,
- complete first problem as example,
- reduce the amount of material on the page,
- allow students to use a word processor for writing and editing,
- allow students to use a calculator,
- shorten the length of the assignment,
- tape written materials, so that the students can follow the reading assignment,
- outline reading material,
- read/tape record tests/quizzes,
- use manipulatives and other physical objects.

(continued on next page)

BLM No. 11 (continued)

Structure study skills:
- teach students how to use an assignment book, with special page(s) for homework,
- provide a daily or weekly homework assignment list,
- vary the assignment for the same objective,
- ask students to repeat directions in own words,
- return corrected assignments with specific comments, as quickly as possible,
- break down assignments into smaller units,
- provide advanced due dates for long term assignments, along with interim deadlines,
- allow students opportunities to provide sample responses,
- teach test-taking skills, e.g., which problems to do first, process of elimination, signal words/directive words,
- teach skimming/scanning skills,
- teach use of table of contents, index, chapter heading, subunit headings, glossary,
- teach previewing skills, questions to ask prior to reading text,
- provide vocabulary lists,
- encourage peer assistance/cooperative learning,
- establish home/school communication system for completion of assignment, upcoming projects,
- provide varied activities for a given concept.

Modify instructional methods:
- use a multi-sensory approach to presenting material,
- consider varied student learning styles when presenting material,
- test orally,
- read test questions,
- use concrete objects/examples to demonstrate concepts,
- provide structure for students to classify information, e.g., outlines, study guides, graphic organizers, webs,
- have students restate/paraphrase information/directions,
- teach students to organize their paperwork/work space,
- grade on material assigned and do not penalize for handwriting/spelling,
- provide student information at her/his desk instead of copying from the board,
- simplify directions, and make them brief,
- allow students to dictate responses to a teacher, peer, or tape recorder,
- display sample of finished products along with directions and materials used,
- allow time at the beginning of the lesson to review previous knowledge in relationship to the new lesson. Allow time at the end to summarize,
- ask factual questions before turning to inferential questioning,
- break tests into segments and use oral testing,
- provide vocabulary before unit is introduced,
- provide essential fact(s) list prior to unit introduction,
- use unconfusing worksheets or black out confusing areas,
- provide discussion questions prior to reading,
- provide transition directions,
- teach and cue key direction words,

(continued on next page)

BLM No. 11 (continued)

- segment directions,
- provide guided practice,
- provide practice trials,
- provide an overview of the material to be presented (e.g., advanced organizers), visual material, interject hands-on tasks,
- use voice change to stress points, repeat important information,
- use humor to keep attention,
- have students orally summarize key points, circulate around the room, model activity desired,
- use large print,
- provide context for the new material,
- use student's prior knowledge both to access and extend the lesson,
- validate the student's past experience/knowledge.

Modify presentation:
- establish a rationale for learning,
- use student's name incorporated into the question,
- incorporate popular themes/characters,
- provide functional link to material,
- ask frequent questions,
- change question level,
- use hand signals to cue behavior,
- alter sequence of presentation,
- repeat major points,
- use verbal cues, e.g., list or number key points, note that which is important,
- change tone of voice to stress points and repeat important information,
- provide anticipation cues,
- provide mnemonic devices.

Testing:
- ask oral multiple choice questions,
- organize test from easy to hard,
- enlarge or highlight key words on test items,
- change response format,
- alter objective criterion level,
- adapt test items for differing response modes,
- use timer to indicate allocated time.

Inclusion: A Service, Not A Place, by Dorothy Kerzner Lipsky and Alan Gartner.

MATRIX OF INSTRUCTIONAL STRATEGIES AND MODIFICATIONS FOR ADDRESSING INDIVIDUAL LEARNING NEEDS & STYLES (LISTED ALPHABETICALLY BY NAME OF ACTIVITY)

The materials that follow were provided by the san Francisco Unified School District, 1999. Reprinted with permission.

Content Standard Area	Strategy/Modification	Need Areas Addressed	Additional Modifications	Learning Styles
✓ LA-reading ✓ LA-writing ✓ LA-oral ✓ Math ✓ Science ✓ Hist/Soc. St.	**Active Note Taking**—Students divide a piece of paper in half. On one side record notes from reading; on the other write comments questions, or reactions.	• Putting ideas together • Selecting key points • Support for reluctant speakers • Focused comprehension • Idea generalization • Organizational skills	• Provide written prompts or questions for students having difficulty generating their own ideas • Partner work • Additional extension questions for GATE • Provide computer template with key words, categories, or phrases	Linguistic Logical Intrapersonal
✓ LA-reading ✓ LA-writing ✓ LA-oral ✓ Math ✓ Science ✓ Hist/Soc. St.	**"Author's" Chair**—Provide regular opportunities for individual students to share a product or assignment with rest of the class or within a small group (writing, read aloud, solve a problem, explain a procedure). Provide all students with an opportunity over time. The audience is encouraged to participate with questions, responses.	• Clarify of identify key process steps • Informal assessment of student understanding or application • Language expression • Auditory support for audience • Sequencing • Student self-assessment	• Allow some students to work with a partner • Work can be "in process" or finished • Allow for different modes of presentation • Allow or require shorter or longer presentation time • Provide audience with guiding questions for comprehension, language development, focus on key information • Video or audio tape student participation	Linguistic Logical Interpersonal Intrapersonal
✓ LA-reading ✓ LA-writing ✓ LA-oral ✓ Math ✓ Science ✓ Hist/Soc. St.	**Brainstorming**—Engage students in brainstorming before they begin to read a selection. Write all words and concepts on board or chart (e.g. possible ways to solve a problem, do a procedure, cause effect, predictions). Tell them to read to see if their ideas are reflected in the text.	• Attention, focus • Idea generation, fluency • Vocabulary development • Sequencing • Focused guide for reading • Key reference points • Making personal connections • Connecting to previous learning	• Record words on cards or in a personal dictionary (ELL) • Make a form on which students can record or have another student record the ideas to support visual/motor difficulties (SLD) • Make large copies and post as a reference (ELL, SLD) • Provide templates with key words or phrases to help students record ideas	Linguistic Spatial Interpersonal Intrapersonal

MATRIX OF INSTRUCTIONAL STRATEGIES AND MODIFICATIONS FOR ADDRESSING INDIVIDUAL LEARNING NEEDS & STYLES (LISTED ALPHABETICALLY BY NAME OF ACTIVITY)

Content Standard Area	Strategy/Modification	Need Areas Addressed	Additional Modifications	Learning Styles
✓ LA-reading ✓ LA-writing ✓ LA-oral Math ✓ Science ✓ Hist/Soc. St.	**Double Entry Journal**—Students divide a sheet of paper in half. On the left side readers identify a passage or quotation of significance in the selection. On the right side, they write their responses, questions, connections, reflections about the passage.	• Language expression • Idea expansion • Key concept identification • format for responding to reading • Connect to personal experiences	• Identify key words, concepts, or passages and prepare in advance to focus learner (at-risk, SLD) • Limited or extend the number of required entries • Use to record important/key concepts from text read • Add section for vocabulary (ELL, SLD at-risk) • Use tables in "word" software to create half of the entries with the learner developing the questions	Linguistic Logical Spatial Kinesthetic Intrapersonal
✓ LA-reading ✓ LA-writing ✓ LA-oral ✓ Math ✓ Science ✓ Hist/Soc. St.	**Expert Group**—(Similar to Jigsaw or Retrieval Charts). Students work in a small group in one area being studied and teach it to other groups. (e.g. expert in one character of a story, historical figure, event, organ, system, etc.)	• Limit/focus area of study • Manage large blocks of information • Taking individual responsibility • Using peer support • Organizing information • Information processing	• Allow for student choice, or to work in an area of strength • Assigned roles for group work • Peer or partner support • Adjust for time needed to complete the task • Provide extended categories or details (GATE) • Additional language experience or vocabulary (ELL)	Linguistic Logical Spatial Musical Kinesthetic Interpersonal Intrapersonal
✓ LA-reading ✓ LA-writing ✓ LA-oral ✓ Math ✓ Science ✓ Hist/Soc. St.	**Focused Question**—When correcting or reviewing student work, let them know that you will be looking for one key feature such as use of descriptive words, subject-verb agreement, steps in a procedure, showing steps in problem solving, etc.	• Attention • Understanding and applying key concepts • Processing information	• Read or show samples from individual student work daily. Focus on key skill or process. • Critique samples of work with whole class or small group	Linguistic Logical Spatial

MATRIX OF INSTRUCTIONAL STRATEGIES AND MODIFICATIONS FOR ADDRESSING INDIVIDUAL LEARNING NEEDS & STYLES (LISTED ALPHABETICALLY BY NAME OF ACTIVITY)

Content Standard Area	Strategy/Modification	Need Areas Addressed	Additional Modifications	Learning Styles
✓ LA-reading ✓ LA-writing ✓ LA-oral ✓ Math ✓ Science ✓ Hist/Soc. St.	**Graphic Organizers**—Use story maps, charts, graphs, character maps, fishbone, Venn diagrams, mind maps, retrieval charts. Use these visual representation of new ideas, review, or to depict information from text read.	• Generate ideas • Expressive language • Organization • Memory • Making connections • Adding detail • Patterns/relationships • Abstract thinking (GATE)	• Use a tape recorder for students who benefit from auditory input • Working with a partner to build language, assist with organization or ideas • Word walls or personal dictionaries for ELL • Use software such as Inspiration to develop outlines/organizational charts	Linguistic Logical Spatial Kinesthetic Intrapersonal
✓ LA-reading ✓ LA-writing ✓ LA-oral ✓ Math ✓ Science ✓ Hist/Soc. St.	**Give One, Get One**—Students list all of the information they know about a specific topic on a sheet of paper. Each student then shares his/her list with at least two other students. As they share, they add one new thing they learn from the other person. The class as a whole then shares lists and teacher or students record facts/information on overhead for class to copy.	• Visual and auditory reinforcement • Memory • Idea generation • Vocabulary development • Making connections • Patterns/relationships	• Teacher can make a final copy for students who may have difficulty (SLD) • Give students the transparency to copy if it is difficult to do from a distance • Share in small groups if attention and movement are difficult for student • Provide specific, guiding questions to focus the generation of ideas	Linguistic Logical Spatial Kinesthetic Musical Interpersonal Intrapersonal
✓ LA-reading ✓ LA-writing ✓ LA-oral ✓ Math ✓ Science ✓ Hist/Soc. St.	**Group Investigation Model**—Students work in cooperative groups. Teacher gives group open-ended discussion questions about a text selection. Students discuss questions, come to consensus and write the answers or present them orally.	• Auditory support • Focus and memory • Vocabulary and concept expansion and acquisition • Self-expression • Active thinking • Making choices or connections	• Teacher monitors or works with individuals or small groups to guide or support the work • Have representative of group report the group response • Use to support problem solving or process work • Assigned peer or partner support • Provide specific rules such as one idea expressed by each student to encourage individual participation	Linguistic Logical Spatial Interpersonal Intrapersonal

MATRIX OF INSTRUCTIONAL STRATEGIES AND MODIFICATIONS FOR ADDRESSING INDIVIDUAL LEARNING NEEDS & STYLES (LISTED ALPHABETICALLY BY NAME OF ACTIVITY)

Content Standard Area	Strategy/Modification	Need Areas Addressed	Additional Modifications	Learning Styles
✓ LA-reading ✓ LA-writing ✓ LA-oral ✓ Math ✓ Science ✓ Hist/Soc. St.	**Interactive Journals**—On one half of a page, the student records notes, key ideas, concepts, concerns, events, connections, procedures from content class. On the other half of the page, the teacher responds with questions, comments, praise, suggestions.	• Receiving and using suggestions and help focus and reinforce key concepts • Memory support • Decision making • Making personal questions • Expanding thinking	• Provide journals to students with predetermined questions, format, size • Adapt size and shape and methods of responses to address individual student needs • Create a list of available questions or prompts to which students can choose or be assigned to respond	Linguistic Logical Spatial Kinesthetic Intrapersonal
✓ LA-reading ✓ LA-writing ✓ LA-oral ✓ Math ✓ Science ✓ Hist/Soc. St.	**KWL**—Model active thinking in the reading of expository text. At the beginning of a lesson, the teacher asks students, as a group, what they already know about a topic. Teacher records the responses. What questions do they want answered or information they want to learn? Can the information be grouped or clustered in any way. After reading or discussion, the students record what they learned.	• Active thinking • Idea generation • Experience building • Connecting to student experiences and prior knowledge • Vocabulary development • Memory support • Visual and auditory support • Preview-readiness for learning	• Use an overhead or chart paper to record responses. Post for reference. • Provide forms on which students can record the information, take notes • Students can work with a partner or in small group to determine what was learned at the end of the lesson • Keep personal dictionary or word list for vocabulary building • Allow extra time for completion • Identify number of responses that are necessary • Do manageable chunks of material at a time	Linguistic Logical Spatial Kinesthetic Musical Interpersonal Intrapersonal
✓ LA-reading ✓ LA-writing ✓ LA-oral ✓ Math ✓ Science ✓ Hist/Soc. St.	**Literature Circles**—Small, temporary groups of students that meet on a regular schedule to discuss their reading. Each group may choose or be assigned a different book to read, based on interest or reading level.	• Engage reluctant readers • Connect to personal experiences and interests • Build auditory capacity and listening skills • Oral expression • Check for understanding • Flexible use of time or comprehension focus	• Provide limited and/or focused questions to assist students in guiding their reading or for discussion • Allow choices of topics/questions discussed (GATE, ELL, SLD) • Provide a variety of book types and levels to accommodate reading skills of students • Use a variety of levels of supplementary reading materials to support learning in content areas	Linguistic Logical Interpersonal Intrapersonal

MATRIX OF INSTRUCTIONAL STRATEGIES AND MODIFICATIONS FOR ADDRESSING INDIVIDUAL LEARNING NEEDS & STYLES (LISTED ALPHABETICALLY BY NAME OF ACTIVITY)

Content Standard Area	Strategy/Modification	Need Areas Addressed	Additional Modifications	Learning Styles
✓ LA-reading ✓ LA-writing ✓ LA-oral ✓ Math ✓ Science ✓ Hist/Soc. St.	**Manipulative and Visual Prompts**—Provide support tools for students in the form of markers, color coded pages, folders, highlighters, post-it notes, reading markers, counting markers, or other manipulatives that assist them in focusing on, organizing, or understanding their work.	• Support visual learning • Focus on key items, words, concepts • Provide opportunities to work with "hands-on" materials • Organization • Memory	• Encourage students to select their own way of organizing their work • Use computer generated organizers or visual tools • Create consistent formats to assist students in organizing their ideas • Allow students generate their own designs or patterns for identifying key ideas	Linguistic Logical Spatial Kinesthetic Intrapersonal
✓ LA-reading ✓ LA-writing ✓ LA-oral ✓ Math ✓ Science ✓ Hist/Soc. St.	**Project Cube**—A project cube is a way to visually present information about a book, text, or other source of content information. On the six sides of the cube, students put words and/or pictures that will tell others about the information learned by the student.	• Summarization • Visualize • Vocabulary development • Making choices • Making connections • Multiple modalities • Focus, selection of key ideas	• Encourage students to use a variety of representations of content knowledge including drawing, music, metaphor, oral presentations, etc. • Make cubes in advance for students as needed. Add questions or key topic on each side • Provide examples and models ad reference point.	Linguistic Logical Spatial Musical Kinesthetic Intrapersonal
✓ LA-reading ✓ LA-writing ✓ LA-oral ✓ Math ✓ Science ✓ Hist/Soc. St.	**Questions First**—Provide questions or step by step directions for an assignment PRIOR to asking students to read or listen. This provides a preparation, readiness, and context for listening or reading.	• Limited focus • Preview • Attention • Comprehension • Order sequencing	• Provide a graphic organizer in advance to help students focus and organize • Adjust type and/or number of questions a student is to answer • Provide choices in how answer or information is to be represented to demonstrate understanding	Linguistic Logical Spatial Intrapersonal
✓ LA-reading ✓ LA-writing ✓ LA-oral ✓ Math ✓ Science ✓ Hist/Soc. St.	**Quick Write**—At key points in a class discussion, procedure, or presentation, students are asked to stop and to a "quick write." This allows students to think about what they have read, heard, or seen and respond to it in their own words. They can include questions or make predictions about what will happen next.	• Clarify thinking • Check comprehension • Use key vocabulary and concepts • Use writing to reinforce reading or listening • Memory reinforcement • Organization	• Create an ongoing and consistent format for Quick Write such as journal, learning log, math or science notebook • Allow for revisions or revisits, or sharing with others • Allow for graphic representation or drawing • Record responses on tape • Use stop and "speak" instead of writing	Linguistic Logical Spatial Kinesthetic Intrapersonal

MATRIX OF INSTRUCTIONAL STRATEGIES AND MODIFICATIONS FOR ADDRESSING INDIVIDUAL LEARNING NEEDS & STYLES (LISTED ALPHABETICALLY BY NAME OF ACTIVITY)

Content Standard Area	Strategy/Modification	Need Areas Addressed	Additional Modifications	Learning Styles
✓ LA-reading ✓ LA-writing ✓ LA-oral ✓ Math ✓ Science ✓ Hist/Soc. St.	**Reciprocal Reading**—Students take turns reading with a partner. At periodic intervals, the listener asks the reader key questions about what was read, such as identifying main idea, summarizing, clarifying, or predicting. Teacher models with students first, then students work in pairs.	• Expressive language • Memory • Information processing • Sequencing • Vocabulary building • Auditory processing • Summarizing	• Use shorter passages for reading if needed • Have a third group member generate questions if it is too difficult for one student to do • Write answers for memory and reinforcement	Linguistic Logical Spatial Intrapersonal
✓ LA-reading ✓ LA-writing ✓ LA-oral ✓ Math ✓ Science ✓ Hist/Soc. St.	**"Relic" Box**—Items related to a specific character, setting, event, topic, or process are placed in a box or bag. The teacher pulls the items from the box one at a time and asks students to predict what it tells them about what will be read or studied. What will happen? What might they learn?	• Experience, language building • Concrete connection to abstract ideas • Making connections • Inference • Attention, focus • Reinforce auditory skills • Kinesthetic and visual modalities	• Students can create their own relic boxed following a book read or at the completion of a unit of study • Use real or representational object • Allow students to see and touch the objects up close	Linguistic Logical Spatial Musical Kinesthetic Interpersonal Intrapersonal
✓ LA-reading ✓ LA-writing ✓ LA-oral ✓ Math ✓ Science ✓ Hist/Soc. St.	**Storyboard**—Have students visually recall or represent major events of a story or chapter. Students use blank copies of a storyboard that has been divided into sections representing the major events, chapters, headings, time periods, etc. Students illustrate in sequence or by heading, the events or key information. Students share storyboard with others.	• Clarify thinking • Sequence • Organizing and classifying • Support and build visual, spatial, and kinesthetic skills • Focus • Identify key ideas • Multiple representations • Reinforcement of ideas	• Prepare a large, class example to serve as a model. Add or reduce number of squares. • Label or identify the types of content to be included • Have students work with a partner or in a small group for support, added ideas, help • Encourage variety of depictions—written, drawn, cut pictures, words, clusters, etc. • Use *Inspiration*, *Power Point*, or a draw program for students to plan their writing or presentation • Assign one topic or square to each member of a group rather than a complete storyboard for each student	Linguistic Logical Spatial Intrapersonal

MATRIX OF INSTRUCTIONAL STRATEGIES AND MODIFICATIONS FOR ADDRESSING INDIVIDUAL LEARNING NEEDS & STYLES (LISTED ALPHABETICALLY BY NAME OF ACTIVITY)

Content Standard Area	Strategy/Modification	Need Areas Addressed	Additional Modifications	Learning Styles
✓ LA-reading ✓ LA-writing ✓ LA-oral ✓ Math ✓ Science ✓ Hist/Soc. St.	**Think Aloud**—The teacher models some of the thinking processes that a good reader engages in when reading. The teacher reads to the students as they follow along with their own copy. The teacher stops throughout the reading to model self-reflection, questioning. Why did the character do this? Why might they act that way? Why was she angry? What might happen next? How do I know? What step do you think will follow? What results might we see? How did I reach this conclusion?	• Information processing • Auditory processing and reinforcement • Check for understanding • Modeling • Verbalization • Vocabulary development • Making connections • Making inferences, applying knowledge	• Students can listen to story or chapter on tape with thinking processes and questions modeled periodically throughout • Students can re-listen to the tape • Use video in the same manner • Students can practice with a partner asking questions • Have a prepared list of questions that can be asked as student reads • Allow sufficient time for student responses, use partners • Tape student reading and personal discussion	Linguistic Logical Musical Interpersonal Intrapersonal
✓ LA-reading ✓ LA-writing ✓ LA-oral ✓ Math ✓ Science ✓ Hist/Soc. St.	**Think-Pair-Share**—Provide students with a question or problem, or reading that is to be analyzed. Ask them to read or think about the answer individually. Share their answer or thoughts with a partner. Agree upon a key idea, answer, or explanation, then share with others in another group or whole class.	• Auditory processing • Listening practice • Identify key concepts • Verbalization • Applying information • Check for understanding • Language development	• Provide a consistent time limit to allow time for each person to share and respond to thinking • Extend time for some students • Allow for responses other than verbally	Linguistic Logical Spatial Interpersonal Intrapersonal

San Francisco Unified School District, 1999, Printed with permission.

INCLUSION ACCOMMODATIONS CHART

Accommodations/ Ideas for students with... → / Online Resources Listed	Learning Strategies	Emotional/ Social/ Behavioral Strategies	Physical/ Perceptual/ Sensory Strategies	Teacher/Student Issues To Address
Above Average Skills www.cectag.org www.nagc.org	Individualize assignments & set realistic/attainable goals	Match maturity level and be age-appropriate	Observe & assess, dependent upon students' needs	Set up classroom centers that address advanced levels
Asperger's www.asperger.org	Structure instruction with routines & use visuals (e.g., lists, graphic organizers)	Guide social skills training during cooperative assignments	Limit distractions & use multi-modal presentations	Draw students back into lessons when they perseverate on own interests
Attention Deficit/ Hyperactivity www.chadd.org	Structure & organize environment with consistency & direct study-skill instruction	Monitor & reinforce positive social interactions	Use active learning and movement	Be aware of possible medication side-effects
Auditory Processing Needs www.ncapd.org/php/	Use written models with verbal instruction; maximize technology	Offer same opportunities as provided to peers	Reinforce eye contact with oral directions	Provide students with additional response time
Autism www.autism-society.org	Select functional vs. more advanced academics (dependent upon cognitive levels)	Present social stories with hypothetical, yet realistic role-playing of interactions with peers	Use tactile stimulation with concrete examples of abstract concepts & visuals	Link students with peer mentors as role models in inclusive environments
Communication Disorders www.asha.org	Give clear explicit directions for assignments with visual aids (e.g., visual dictionaries, videos, computer graphics)	Include students in all social class groups; be aware of frustrations	Face students when speaking; use conversational tone; ask students to paraphrase	Collaborate with speech pathologist
Conduct disorders www.nmha.org www.nimh.nih.gov/	Structure class environment with clear rules outlined & enforced	Use behavioral contracts; student meta-cognition; realistic praise & positive reinforcement	Check students' perceptions (e.g., diary, log of thoughts, student-teacher conferences)	Communicate with parents concerning students' behavioral strides

(continued on next page)

Deafness/Hearing Loss www.agbell.org www.hearingloss.org www.deafchildren.org	Optimize students' abilities (e.g., more visuals, outlines, copies of teacher's guides & lessons	Provide opportunities to socialize with peers in class & extracurricular activities	Match technology with student needs (e.g., PECS system, interactive board for easier note-taking)	Be aware of individual preferences (e.g., total communication, speaking, lip reading, finger spelling, and/or signing)
Depression www.nimh.nih.gov/	Allow alternate assignments/ assessments if academic performance is negatively influenced by emotions	Have available feel-good emotional outlets (e.g., intersperse exercise, art, and/or music with learning)	Encourage meta-cognition for students to accurately reflect on perceptions & trigger points (e.g., graph daily moods)	Monitor quieter students who reach out in silent ways (e.g., writings, art, absences, self-care, dress)
Developmental Disabilities/ Intellectual Disabilities www.devdelay.org/ www.thearc.org	Use concrete, step-by-step teaching with modeling & repetition; concentrate on functional academics	Use age-appropriate activities; reward approximations toward learning goals; teach social skills	Communicate with school nurse regarding any medical concerns	Relate learning to individual interests and have high expectations
Dyslexia www.learningally.org www.interdys.org www.ortonacademy.org	Use multi-sensory, systematic, direct phonetic skill instruction across curriculum areas (e.g., breaking up more difficult multi-syllabic vocabulary words)	Do not embarrass students by asking them to read in front of peers; allow wait time; increase praise for reading progress; use age appropriate materials	Increase individual student awareness of letter reversals (e.g., self-corrections; use highlighters, allow students to use a ruler); enlarge text	Use technology to ease frustrations (e.g., books on tape, Recording for the Blind and Dyslexic)
Obsessive Compulsive Disorder www.ocfoundation.org www.adaa.org	Channel concerns for perfection & ritualistic behavior into appropriate academic/ behavioral tasks	Intervene using personalized strategies, (e.g., behavioral monitoring, quiet signals)	Be aware of possible behavioral triggers, physical effects & emotional stress	Advocate understanding and accepting environments that do not ridicule students
Oppositional Defiant Disorder www.nmha.org www.mentalhealth.com	Empower students by giving acceptable learning direction/ choices (e.g., choose 3 of these 5 listed assignments)	"Like" the child, but "dislike" the behavior; try to establish ongoing, nonjudgmental & trusting relationships	Check students' sensory perceptions for accuracy by asking them to paraphrase rules and interactions	Do not engage in power struggles with students, but be firm, consistent, and fair

(continued on next page)

Physical Impairment www.ucpa.org http://specialed.about.com	Realize that physical difficulties and learning deficits are not synonymous; use assistive technology	Allow students same access and opportunities to meaningfully participate in all activities with peers	Communicate with physical, occupational, and/or speech therapists to coordinate strategies	Ease physical, fine and/or gross motor requirements, but do not dilute academic assignments
Specific Learning Disability www.ldanatl.org www.ncld.org	Use task-analysis to determine how to proceed and tailor remediation; challenge students but do not frustrate	Increase social skills and class cohesiveness by varying direct skill instruction with cooperative learning	Address letter reversals, auditory processing, visual and/or fine motor weaknesses	Appeal to untapped strengths and interests to motivate students and boost self-esteem
Twice Exceptional http://www.uniquelygifted.org/	Vary types of instruction and assessments, using multiple intelligences & brain-based learning principles	Reward both growth and accomplishments, honoring unique social/behavioral/emotional/academic levels	Address various sensory, physical & perceptual needs	Concentrate on growth and strengths versus a deficit paradigm
Visual Impairments/ Blindness www.afb.org www.rfbd.org	Appeal to auditory and kinesthetic/tactile modalities with increased written directions; use learning manipulatives	Include students in all activities with peer education about students' visual needs, interests, and strengths	Remove physical barriers in the classroom & school environment; work with mobility trainers	Optimize assistive technology (e.g., talking websites, tactile outlines)

Sources:

Karten, T. (2010). *Inclusion strategies that work: Research-based methods for the classroom.* Thousand Oaks, CA: Corwin Press.

Karten, T. (2009). *Inclusion succeeds with effective strategies, Grades K-5* (laminated reference guide). Port Chester, New York: Dude Publishing. Used with author's permission.

6
Cooperative Learning, Peer Supports, and Social-Emotional Learning

What is cooperative learning?
Cooperative learning enables students, including those with disabilities, to be involved in and benefit from the school's instructional program. Cooperative learning is more than putting students into small groups. It shifts the roles of both the students and the teachers. Students become more active participants and less passive recipients, while teachers take on more of a role of coach or facilitator. Cooperative learning may be considered a supplementary aid and service; it was selected by teachers in the NCERI study as the most important instructional tool in support of inclusive education. Cooperative learning warrants special attention for the following additional reasons:

- there is a strong research base as to its positive outcomes for both general and special education students;
- there is a well-developed body of literature on its implementation across classrooms, grade levels, and subject matter;
- it is commonly used in general education classrooms and familiar to regular education teachers;
- it is the most frequently used strategy in general education classrooms with special education students, i.e., inclusive classrooms;
- it actively engages each of the students, in different roles; and
- its design is intrinsically inclusive.

There are several different designs of cooperative learning. Some serve as an adjunct within a broader curricula framework while, in other designs, cooperative learning is a key feature of a comprehensive reform plan. Common to all of the programs that have shown significant gains for students are two complementary features: promoting interdependence within the groups, by having the partners work together to accomplish the goal; and holding students individually accountable for demonstrating their mastery of the knowledge or skill. Each design considers interpersonal and small group skills as important.

How does cooperative learning relate to the law?
Although not mentioned specifically in federal education law, cooper-ative learning is a support to carry out IDEA and NCLB's requirements. It does so by enabling students to make progress toward annual goals, be involved in and make progress in the general curriculum, and be educated and participate with students who do not have a disability. Cooperative learning, inclusion, and broader school reform are part of an integral whole.

> Cooperative learning is good for all students and... it is a part of comprehensive school reform efforts. To achieve this reform, teachers must work together to build networks within their school community. Teachers must also establish a cooperative classroom ethic that emphasizes overall community building, open communication about differences and classroom practices, and reciprocal helping relationships. Meaningful content in cooperative lessons is critical for the success of all students. For students to succeed within their groups, careful consideration regarding group heterogeneity must be given in conjunction with roles that ensure active, equal participation by all students. Creative assessment practices must be developed to document achievement of meaningful outcomes for students. All these considerations require planning and structure in order for the teaching to be successful.[38]

What are "best practices" of cooperative learning?
There are a number of cooperative learning "systems." A review of the literature on this topic in the Harvard Education Letter (May/June 2000) indicates that the various systems differ in the following ways: the amount of structure provided; the kinds of rewards offered; the methods used to hold students individually accountable; and the use of group competition. Among the major systems the Harvard Education Letter identifies are the following:

Student Learning Team (SLT): Developed initially by Bob Slavin at Johns Hopkins University, the emphasis in SLT is on team goals and team success. There are several SLT programs, some used across different grades and subjects, while others are specific to math (grades 3–6) and reading and writing (grades 3–5).

Learning Together: Developed at the University of Minnesota by David Johnson and Roger Johnson, it features four or five-member heterogeneous groups working together on a common assignment. A single product is produced and the group receives a reward together. Emphasis is on team-building activities and how well the group works together.

Jigsaw: Developed initially as a way to replace competition with cooperation in the classroom, students are divided into "jigsaw groups," each with five or six members, diverse in terms of gender, ethnicity, race, and ability. Each member is given a segment of the assigned material to study. Once familiar with the material, members of each group who had the same assigned segment regroup in an "expert group," where they discuss the assigned material and prepare for their presentation to the "jigsaw group." Members return to their "jigsaw group" and each presents/teaches a segment to the whole group. Members are encouraged to ask questions for understanding and the teacher rotates among the groups. The unit is completed with a quiz on the material.

Kagan Structures: An eclectic approach that addresses the achievement of standards for all in heterogenous classrooms using cooperative learning. Material is available covering English and Language Arts, Mathematics, Science, and Social Studies, with particular adaptations for students with disabilities and English as Second Language Learners. A number of cooperative learning strategies have been developed by Kagan. They appear below:

Cooperative learning strategies[39]
Round robin: Each student shares something with classmates.

Corners: Teacher presents four alternatives; students divide into four groups and move to corners of the room. Students discuss and then listen to and paraphrase ideas from other groups.

Pairs check: Students work in pairs within groups of four. In pairs, students alternate as one solves a problem while the other coaches. After every two problems, one pair checks to see if they have the same answer as the other pair.

Think-pair share: Students think to themselves about a teacher provided topic; they then pair up with another student to discuss it, and then share their thoughts with the whole class.

Team word-webbing: Students write simultaneously on a piece of chart paper, drawing main concepts and supporting elements and bridges.

Co-op: Students work in groups to produce a group product to share with the whole class; each student makes a contribution to the group.

Jigsaw: Each student becomes an expert on one topic by working with members from other teams that are assigned the corresponding topic. Upon returning to the team, each one in turn teaches the group on the expert topic. All students are assessed on all aspects of the topic.

What is peer support?

In many ways, cooperative learning is a form of peer support. Peer support programs also can have a social interaction focus as well as an instructional one (e.g., peer-mediated instruction[40]). Among the socially-focused programs are buddy programs, pal groups, and Circle of Friends. While sometimes called "natural supports," they are intentional efforts to expand the social network of students with disabilities. Experience in many schools is that such activities become the basis for ongoing relationships among students, both in school and in the community.

What are "best practices" of peer support?

Among instructionally-based peer programs are peer initiated training, peer monitoring, and peer tutoring. Some peer tutoring programs involve students without disabilities tutoring students with disabilities. Student tutors expand the resource of those providing instruction, as well as offer opportunities for disabled and nondisabled students to work together. Utley (2001) says that peer–mediated instruction addresses the important classroom question of differentiating instruction. She asserts that peer-mediated instruction and interventions;

> may serve as an effective strategy that (a) facilitates the inclusion of students with disabilities into general education classroom settings, (b) enhances academic achievement on standardized tests and curriculum-specific measures, (c) improves inter-personal relationships and the acceptance of individual differences among diverse students, and (d) improves student discipline in a proactive and positive manner.[41]

Maheady et al. (2001) summarize two earlier literature reviews[42] of peer mediated instruction and intervention (PMII), particularly for students with mild disabilities. The 1991 review reported that PMII produced noticeable pupil improvements in three distinct yet interrelated domains, i.e., academic, interpersonal, personal/social development.

> Peer-teaching systems worked because they created more learner-friendly instructional environments. That is, they established more favorable pupil-teacher ratios within the classroom, increased student on-task time and response opportunities, provided additional opportunities for pupils to receive positive and corrective feedback, and enhanced pupils' opportunities to receive individualized help and encouragement. Moreover, students have consistently preferred peer-teaching practices over more traditional instructional arrangements, i.e., teacher-led and student-regulated activities.[43]

The 1997 survey, after confirming the positive effects that PMII has on pupils' basic academic skills, reported that:

> PMII components are highly effective for students with special needs because they allow teachers to individualize instruction on a classwide basis, and the academic and social benefits associated with such programs can be extended to nondisabled pupils in the same settings. Utley et al. suggested further that PMII may also provide an effective and efficient method for minimizing the excessive workloads that presently confront general education teachers. For example, peer monitoring procedures may assist in the correction and feedback process; peer modeling, tutoring, and group-oriented contingencies may facilitate the development of pupil's social skills without additional time allocations; and positive social networks might greatly enhance the general classroom climate in many schools.[44]

Bringing the findings up-to-date, Maheady et al. (2001) report on a ClassWide Peer-Assisted Self-Management (CWPASM) program that improved student behaviors and class climate; ClassWide Peer Tutoring (CWPT) that showed powerful academic effects in second language acquisition and literacy[45]; Peer-Assisted Learning Strategies (PALS) that addressed literacy and mathematics instruction to facilitate the successful inclusion of students with mild disabilities in general education settings[46]; Classwide Student Tutoring Teams (CSTT) which produced substantial academic gains (e.g., all students with disabilities obtained passing grades) in the mathematics performance of students with mild disabilities enrolled in general education settings.[47]

Additional power is gained when disabled students are offered the opportunity themselves to be tutors. A recent meta-analysis provides support for designs that involve students with disabilities as tutors.[48] This may take the form of a cross-age model, where older students with a disability tutor younger children without a disability. Here, the student with a disability gains the benefit of learning through teaching. Factors contributing to the power of such a design include: the status of being recognized as someone who is able to give (not always receive) help and take responsibility, and, as such, being viewed as someone who is capable of achievement and worthy of respect.[49] Additionally this design provides the opportunity to review material as one prepares to tutor and to focus on learning as the tutor seeks to connect with the tutee.[50] Students with any disability can assume the tutor role. An interesting design has been developed in New Orleans where older students with emotional disturbance/behavior disorders serve as mentors to younger at-risk protegees.[51]

When all students have a chance to play the role of both tutor and tutee, a pro-learning atmosphere, one which is cooperative and collegial, is more likely to develop in the classroom. Collaborative designs reject deficit-based education models, that promote segregated dual systems. Instead, they provide the basis for restructuring education systems to develop programs that serve all students together, and serve them well.

Drawing from the theoretical work of Jean Piaget and Lev Vygotsky, Harry Stack Damon (1984) summarizes the case for all students being involved.

> Because peer tutoring is of demonstrable value both to tutor and tutee, an ideal school approach would expose children to both roles. Any child has an area of competence that can be imparted to a younger or less sophisticated child. Conversely, all children can benefit from tutoring in areas in which they are relative novices. In assuming both tutor and tutee roles, children not only gain the benefits of tutee as well as tutor, but also a highly informative experience in role reversal. The child's switching from expert to novice can impart to the child deeper and more sympathetic understanding of the educational endeavor.[52]

While peer programs often develop on an informal basis, those that are most effective are planned and structured. In some school districts, which have community service requirements, peer support activities are incorporated. Training of tutors is a valuable component of peer support programs. A junior high school peer buddies program in West Feliciana Parish, LA, included disability awareness as part of the training, as it set clear guidelines for the buddies (e.g., don't talk down to the student, don't provide help without being asked, don't coddle the student with a disability, don't treat her/him like a child). A Virginia peer program emphasized the importance of praise that is specific to performance, including reinforcement for successful performance.

The benefits for the "tutor" can be both cognitive and affective. In the cognitive domain, a review in the Harvard Education Letter reported that "tutors learn at least as much as the students they teach—and tutors who are far behind academically gain even more."[53] For the tutors, tutoring offers the opportunity to practice activities in which learning has occurred but mastery has not yet been achieved or those in which learning is not yet generalized to other settings. Tutors learn by reviewing, reinforcing, reformulating the material from another setting, as well as learning from a different vantage point. First characterized as "learning through teaching" in programs developed in the 1960s,[54] the idea of involving students with disabilities in the tutor role was introduced in the 1970s.[55] One of the first of these programs was conducted in Central Harlem by the New Careers Training Laboratory, then at Queens College, The City University of New York. Both tutors and tutees gained academic, behavioral, and social skills. A decade later, Brigham Young University conducted a three-year project, "Handicapped Children as Tutors." Students with mental retardation and those with learning disabilities tutored both similarly disabled and nondisabled students. Research findings on the project found that:

- handicapped children functioned effectively as tutors. They can learn to demonstrate instructional content, monitor tutee performance, and give appropriate feedback.
- both tutors and tutees experienced growth in the topic tutored.
- parents, teachers, and tutees perceived reverse-role tutoring as an effective intervention strategy in special education.[56]

The following is a report from an 11th grade non-disabled student who served as a peer assistant, teaching students about weight lifting as part of meeting a service requirement in a Howard County (MD) school. It illustrates the affective benefits for the non-disabled tutor.

> It's difficult for me to express what I have learned because working with significantly impaired special education students has changed me and changed my life for the better in a way that I can't communicate. When I signed up for this class, I took it because I needed an easy elective to pull up my GPA. I never guessed that I would end up working so much and so hard. I never guessed I could care so deeply about anyone or anything.
>
> Before I became an aide, I came to school late every day. This is because I was so focused on being at every party, drinking as much as I could and cruising around in my car faster than I should whenever possible. That was my life. I didn't care about school. Now, I have people who need me. I've had to change my life style. I want to go to college and major in special education now. Before, my parents wanted me to go to college but I didn't care. I really didn't think I was good enough to make it in college either. I have discovered that I can really make a difference in the lives of these kids. I felt a responsibility to be a better person, to work harder and to learn more.
>
> I know a lot of teachers think guys like me don't deserve to be an aide. They think it should be a job reserved for GT [Gifted & Talented] people. I guess they don't believe all that stuff they preach about seeing people as a glass half filled instead of half empty. I'm starting to believe that stuff too. About the intensity five students, and even about myself.
>
> I have also discovered that I have guts I didn't know I had. When the guys use the word 'retard' as an insult, I know now that it's a disability, not an insult. I feel so sick when they say that I can't just play along with the gag anymore. I have to speak up now. I've become an advocate. I am not sure how this happened to me; it wasn't something I ever thought I could do.
>
> [I] think having these students in regular classes has made our school a better place. I think it has made people think. One day a bunch of us guys were talking about what it would be like to have kids of our own. We all had our TV sitcom ideas about what it would be like. And then we thought about what it would be like if our kid was born with mental retardation. That was really heavy stuff to talk about! Maybe its normal for the smart honor student types to sit around and worry about real life but for me and my dumb jock-type friends to get that serious is scary! This school is really different since this program came to town. It made everybody have to become better people than we were before the program.[57]

What are the roles of administrators regarding cooperative learning and peer mediated learning?

Both cooperative learning and peer mediated learning are activities that can take place within a single teacher's classroom; as such, they need no special administrative arrangements. Opportunities for professional development may be necessary, especially to familiarize teachers with the various cooperative learning and peer mediated designs. A significant aspect of the training is the role change for teachers, from being the sole dispenser of knowledge to organizing and facilitating students as active providers of knowledge to their peers. When cooperative learning and peer mediated learning activities are a common feature of the general education classroom, the IEP Team can rely upon them as a "natural" support for a student with disabilities. Otherwise, their use may be incorporated as a specific supplementary aid in the student's IEP. Should this be a strategy with which the general education teacher is not familiar, professional development for the teacher can be incorporated in the student's IEP.

Well-designed and carefully implemented, cooperative learning and peer mediated learning may dissipate parental and teacher concerns as to the twin pitfalls of failing to engage the student for whom the material is quickly understood or the student who needs more time or greater depth. Cooperative learning lessons where everyone performs the same activity fail to tap the richness of the strategy. Tasks can be differentiated by quantity as well as complexity, so as to appropriately engage all learners.

An example of such a lesson:
> In a "jigsaw" activity, designed for heterogeneous groups of four or five, each student reads a segment of a succinct biography of Harriet Tubman. Students with special needs review a relatively short segment of the book with a resource teacher before the class assignment. Students able to comprehend more complex material read a more demanding section of the book. Other students receive portions that appropriately challenge them. Students summarize their reading, report to one another, review their findings together, and are responsible for knowing information about all aspects of Tubman's life. Students demonstrate their knowledge by answering the teacher's questions, completing a group project, taking a quiz, or performing a skit. Each person's contribution, no matter its complexity, is essential for the group to be successful.[58]

Similarly, as discussed above, well-designed and conducted peer mediated learning programs benefit both tutor and tutee. This is especially the case when students have the opportunity to play both roles.

What is Social Emotional Learning (SEL)?

Using the description from the Collaborative for Academic, Social, and Emotional Learning (CASEL), social emotional learning is the process of developing the skills to recognize and manage emotions, develop caring and concern for others, establish positive relationships, and make responsible decisions. These skills have been shown to be significant in children's overall development, especially as it relates to their health, ethical character, citizenship, academic learning, and motivation. For schools SEL provides a focus for strong personal development, healthy lifestyles, prevention of behavioral problems, and greater focus on learning.

CASEL, founded over eighteen years ago, is a resource for educators who wish to incorporate SEL into their school and/or classroom programs. Their current primary focus is to provide practitioners with tools, guidelines, and support to enhance SEL programming. In response to the need of the educational community to demonstrate effectiveness of all initiatives, CASEL is now looking to identify and/or create tools that can be use to document SEL-related student outcomes.

The core elements of SEL are based upon the original work of Peter Salovey and Jack Mayer in the early 1990's, and subsequently popularized by Daniel Goleman in his 1995 book, *Emotional Intelligence: Why It Can Be More Important Than IQ*. The application of emotional intelligence to the schools is captured in the video production of 1996 entitled *Emotional Intelligences: A New Vision for Educators*, produced by National Professional Resources, Inc.

The significance of emotional intelligences skills is related to the child in his school, family, and community and later to the adult world and workplace. The reality of this was discussed in 1990 in the Secretary's Commission on Achieving Necessary Skills, known as the SCANS report of the Department of Labor, and is an ongoing topic in the writing and presentations of Daniel Goleman.

Regardless of the specifics of the program implemented by a school or district, the goals are usually the same: to assist in the development of sound character and human civility through collaborative involvement of students, educators, parents, and community members.

What are the best practices of SEL?

As innovations in education have continued, and challenges to today's youth increased, a number of programs/focuses have been developed which fall under the broad umbrella of SEL. These may include, but are not limited to, programs such as:

- Character Education
- Service Learning

- Drug and Alcohol Prevention
- Bullying Prevention
- Conflict Resolution
- Social Skills Development
- Teen Pregnancy Prevention
- Decision Making/Problem Solving

Character education programs have proliferated in recent years. Led in large measure by Thomas Lickona, author of *Educating for Character* and *Character Matters,* these programs provide schools with specific lessons and ideas for incorporating character education activities into core curriculum. This can be most seamlessly achieved in the areas of language arts/literature and social studies/history. Other programs have a school-wide impact and feature specific traits/attributes/virtues such as respect, responsibility, honesty, etc. Most of these programs have a parent component so that there is reinforcement across the child's whole day, both home and school. The most common reference in these programs is the Golden Rule!

One of the most notable resources for character education in the schools emanates from the Cooperating School Districts of St. Louis, Missouri. Founded in the late 1980's by a group of educators, parents, and business leaders, their project, known as CHARACTERplus, works to advance character education programming and sustain its impact throughout the region. It addresses issues related to responsibility, student character and academic achievement by providing quality training, leadership, and resources. It also has national prominence due to a conference it supports every summer. Additional information about the program can be found at www.characterplus@csd.org.

Emotional literacy programs are also receiving much attention. One such program is *Emotional Literacy in the Middle School.* Authored by Maurer, Brackett, and Plain, this program engages the intellectual, emotional, and social aspects of the student by incorporating activities such as self-reflection, analysis, classroom discussion, family interaction, and creative writing assignments into the curriculum. Students learn to recognize, label, understand, and experience their own feelings and actions, as well as those of others. An elementary version of this program will be available in Fall 2007.

Another new resource in the SEL field is a research-validated curriculum that focuses on teaching skills that will enable students to be reflective, non-impulsive, and responsible decision makers and problem solvers while emphasizing critical thinking skills. Entitled *Social Decision Making/Social Problem Solving (SDM/SPS)* this program impacts student behavior, academic learning, and social/emotional life. It promotes a multicultural perspective by building group cohesion, acceptance of differences, and the ability to understand different points of view. The activities build skills such as self-control, listening, respectful communication, how to give and receive help, and how to work cooperatively and fairly in groups. The program uses a wide range of cooperative learning methods, such as small-group brainstorming, problem solving, and role-playing activities. There are three volumes, Grades 2–3, 4–5, 6–8, and each includes assessment tools for tracking progress and numerous reproducible worksheets.[59] The lead author for this series is Dr. Maurice Elias, one of the foremost proponents and respected authorities in the field of social emotional learning.

Further information on the above initiatives is extremely plentiful. An excellent source of specifics related to SEL is the CASEL website: www.CASEL.org. The website www.NPRinc.com has a great number of staff development and classroom resources for review and purchase.

Where can I find additional information about cooperative learning? Peer mediated learning? SEL?

For information about specific cooperative learning "systems," the following are available:

Aranha, Mary. *A Good Place To Be: A Leadership Guide for Making Your Vision a Reality . . . Within Your School, Within Your Classroom, Within Your Family, Within Your Heart.* Port Chester, NY: Dude Publishing, 2002.

Bender, W.N. and Shores, C. *Response to Intervention: A Practical Guide for Every Teacher.* Thousand Oaks, CA: Corwin Press, 2007.

Casbarro, J. *RTI Classroom Reference Guide.* Port Chester NY: Dude Publishing, 2008.

Cohen, Jonathan. *Educating Minds and Hearts: Social Emotional Learning and the Passage into Adolescence.* New York, NY: Teachers College Press, 1999.

Council for Exceptional Children, *Position on Response to Intervention (RTI). The Unique Role of Special Education and Special Educators.* Arlington VA, 2007.

Elias, Maurice & Harriett Arnold. *The Educator's Guide to Emotional Intelligence and Academic Achievement.* Thousand Oaks, CA: Corwin Press, 2006.

Elias, Maurice & Joseph E. Zins, et al. *Promoting Social & Emotional Learning Guidelines for Educators.* Alexandria, VA: ASCD, 1997.

Fuchs, D., Fuchs, L.S., and Vaughn, S. (Eds.) *Response to Intervention: A Framework for Educators.* Newark, DE: International Reading Association, 2008.

Gardner, Howard. How Are Kids Smart? (Video) Port Chester, NY: National Professional Resources, Inc., 1996.

Glass, K.T. *Lesson Design for Differentiated Instruction, Grades 4-9.* Thousand Oaks, CA: Corwin Press, 2009.

Goleman, Daniel. *Emotional Intelligence: A New Vision for Educators* (Video). Port Chester, NY: National Professional Resources, Inc., 1996.

Goleman, Daniel. *Emotional Intelligence: Why It Can Matter More Than IQ*. New York, NY: Bantam Books, 1995.

Gorman, Jean Cheng. *Emotional Disorders and Learning Disabilities in the Classroom: Interactions and Interventions.* Thousand Oaks, CA: Corwin Press, 2001.

Kagan, Spencer & Laurie Kagan. *Reaching Standards Through Cooperative Learning: Providing for ALL Learners in General Education Classrooms* (4-video series). Port Chester, NY: National Professional Resources, Inc., 1999.

Kagan, Spencer & Miguel Kagan. *Multiple Intelligences: The Complete MI Book.* San Clemente, CA: Kagan Cooperative Learning, 1998.

Kemp, K.A. *Peer to Peer Instruction in the Classroom* (laminated reference guide). Port Chester, NY Dude Publishing, 2009.

Lickona, Thomas. *Character Matters.* New York, NY: Touchstone, 2004.

Lickona, Thomas. *Educating for Character: How Our Schools Can Teach Respect and Responsibility.* New York, NY: Bantam, 1992.

Mastropieri, M/A., Scruggs, T.E., and Berkeley, S.L., *Peers Helping Peers,* Educational Leadership, 64 (5), 54-58.

Putnam, Joanne W. *Cooperative Learning and Strategies for Inclusion.* Baltimore, MD: Paul H. Brookes Publishing, 1998.

Ryan, Kevin & Karen E. Bohlin. *Building Character in Schools: Practical Ways to Bring Moral Instruction to Life.* San Francisco, CA: Jossey-Bass, 2003.

Salovey, Peter. *Optimizing Intelligences: Thinking, Emotion, and Creativity* (Video). Port Chester, NY: National Professional Resources, Inc., 1998.

Snell, Martha E. & Rachel Janney. *Social Relationships & Peer Support.* Baltimore, MD: Paul H. Brookes Publishing Co., Inc., 2000.

Stirling, Diane, G. Archibald, L. McKay & S. Berg. *Character Education Connections for School, Home and Community: A Guide for Integrating Character Education.* Port Chester, NY: National Professional Resources, Inc., 2001.

Thousand, Jacqueline S., Richard A. Villa & Ann I. Nevin. *Creativity and Collaborative Learning: The Practical Guide to Empowering Students, Teachers, and Families, 2nd Edition.* Baltimore, MD: Paul H. Brookes Publishing, 2002.

Tomlinson, C.A., Brimpin, K. & Narvaez, L. *The Differentiated School: Making Revolutionary Changes in Teaching and Learning.* Alexandria VA: Association for Supervision and Curriculum Development, 2008.

Wright, J. *RTI and Classroom Behaviora* (laminated reference guide). Port Chester, NY: Dude Publishing, 2011.

7
Interventions: Academic and Behavioral

The plight of struggling learners is one of the foremost challenges of our educational system. Whether the reason be academic or behavioral, it is essential that, before these students become casualties of our schools, today's educators be prepared to address them through the implementation of very specific strategies that are matched to their unique needs. In the academic area one such process is know as Response To Intervention (RTI); in the behavioral area such a process is known as Positive Behavioral Intervention Supports (PBIS). In both cases, intervention is a term used to describe a change in instruction, either learning or behavioral, with the goal of improving student performance and achieving adequate student progress. Each of these models offers earlier, more relevant help for students at-risk of academic or behavioral problems, and each provides critical information about instructional needs of the students that can be used to create effective educational interventions.

The importance of effective instruction for all students in general education is so critical that districts *are permitted* to use up to 15% of their special education dollars to improve the impact of general education; however, if disproportionality exits, then the districts *must* use the 15% to make general education more effective.

In an attempt to look at academics and behavior from a school-wide perspective, and to determine the "how, when and for whom" specific interventions need to be directed, a three-tier pyramid model is often presented. This is not a lock-step process but rather a framework that encourages districts and schools to creatively respond to the students for whom they are responsible. Additionally, schools can share expertise between the team that focuses on the academic issues, often referred to as the Academic Support Team (or something very similar) and that which focuses on behaviors, often referred to as the PBIS team. The whole school then becomes accountable for and focused on supports and results. Within this model, the entire student body is provided with a solid curriculum, effective instruction and positive behavioral supports.

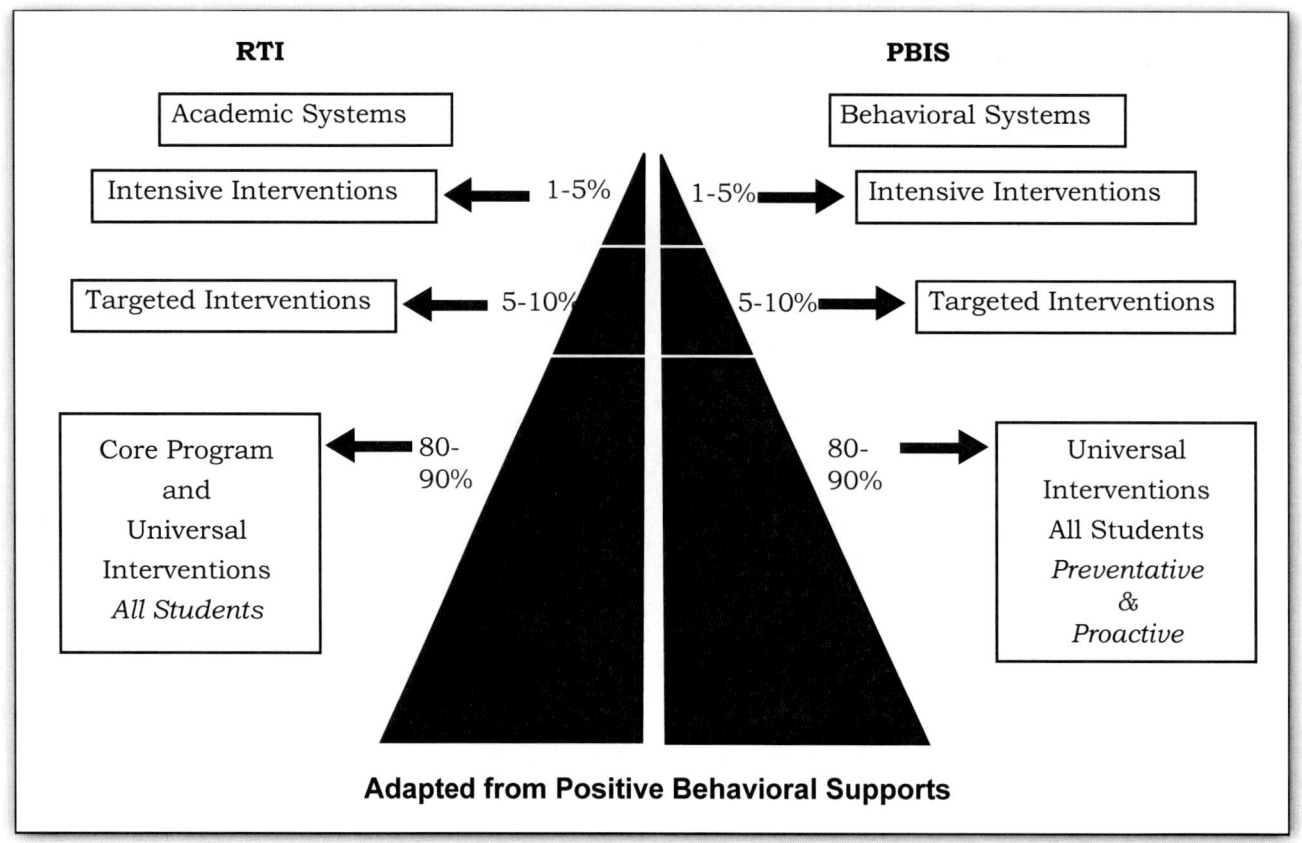

Adapted from Positive Behavioral Supports

Tier I Universal
This tier is generally viewed as the core or universal program that is offered to all students, with differentiated instruction provided to address student variability. Opportunities for students to benefit from a rich curriculum that is presented in a variety of ways are critical at this tier, as are general well-defined classroom management strategies. RTI's bedrock premise is the presence of solid, high-quality classroom instruction for all students.

In both the academic and behavioral areas it is predicted that between 80% and 90% of students will respond at Tier I and be well served.

Tier II Supplemental and Targeted
This level includes more intensive and targeted interventions. These are provided in addition to instruction in the general education curriculum and implementation of an overall classroom management structure. Usually a multi-disciplinary team assists in determining what is necessary to match with a particular student need, and then a plan, with a specific intervention that is closely monitored, is developed to target a deficit. This is usually short term and lasts for six weeks or longer, depending on the results as evidenced by the data. In this tier, students can be grouped for an intervention as long as the deficit area for all in the group is similar, and the intervention is appropriately targeted.

This tier represents about 5% to 10% of the population. Students who progress well at this level may return to Tier I while those who do not demonstrate sufficient progress may be recommended for a new intervention. Or, if the team feels more intensive intervention is needed, they may be referred to Tier III.

Tier III Intensive
This tier is for that very small percentage of students, usually between only 1-5%, for whom individualized and intensive interventions are needed. These students are often those eligible for special services under IDEA. The abundance of information and data from Tier I and Tier II interventions becomes a very valuable part of a referral packet. More comprehensive evaluation may be necessary to ensure that the skill deficit areas are appropriately targeted, and that the students are provided with the appropriate services for which they are eligible.

Response To Intervention (RTI)
RTI holds great potential for schools today. Through its focus on the delivery of evidence-based interventions and its use of student response to those interventions as a basis for determining instructional needs and their intensity, RTI provides a roadmap that is both an opportunity and a challenge for all educators. Simply stated, RTI is a process for providing systematic, research-based instruction and interventions to students who are experiencing difficulties learning. It is based upon an assumption that the needs of the students are being appropriately targeted and that there is continuous monitoring of progress. Its primary use to date has been related to literacy development but the process is just as applicable for any other core content area. However, there is little information or research in areas beyond reading.

Utilizing a multi-step approach, RTI provides services and interventions to students who are experiencing difficulty with learning. Progress made at each point in the instructional process is monitored, and results of this are used to make decisions about the need for additional and/or different interventions. With this data it is also possible to keep everyone, including the student if appropriate, aware of progress. Perhaps one of the most positive benefits of RTI is its ability to limit the amount of academic failure students experience by intervening at early stages. It safeguards against the negative effects of delaying intervention until there is such a deficit that it is almost impossible for the student to "catch up."

Additional benefits and features of the RTI process are that it:
- responds to the provisions in both IDEA 2004 and NCLB related to providing additional support for struggling students;
- functions primarily as a general education initiative that addresses students early in their educational experience;

- requires general education and special education to work together as a seamless system;
- provides data needed to identify those students who are not reaching established benchmarks/standards/goals, through the use of universal screening, administered multiple times during the school year;
- presumes the use of a problem-solving model in which a multi-disciplinary team uses progress monitoring and data analysis for decision-making;
- utilizes interventions that are systematically applied, based upon research-based practices, and that are closely monitored by data collection and review;
- can replace the I.Q. discrepancy model for determining the presence of a learning disability;
- potentially reduces the number of students who are mistakenly identified as learning disabled;
- reduces the overall number of students who are referred for special education services while increasing the number of students who are successfully served in general education;
- limits unnecessary testing that has little or no instructional value.

Based upon NCLB's focus on accountability, RTI includes the following components:

1. High-quality, culturally-responsive classroom instruction
 —Students receive at least 90 minutes a day of core reading instruction in their assigned classrooms (as well as core math and science instruction), delivered by teachers who are highly-qualified according to NCLB.

2. Scientifically-Based Reading Research (SBRR)
 —Reading instruction/curriculum reflects the research on how children learn to read and how teachers can assist struggling readers. For reading, this includes systematic, direct instruction in its five primary components: phonemic awareness, phonics, fluency, vocabulary, and comprehension.

3. Universal screening
 —A process used early in the academic year to identify those students who are at risk of not meeting grade level standards; tools such as Curriculum Based Measurement (CBM) and/or direct assessment, (i.e., fluency probes, DIBELS, AIMSweb, Skill Builders, etc.) are used to identify student proficiency levels and rate of learning. Students who do not meet established benchmarks as demonstrated through these tools, become candidates for classroom interventions.

4. Continuous progress monitoring
 —A scientifically-based practice used to assess student academic performance, evaluate the effectiveness of their instruction and

make decisions for future instruction and/or interventions. It provides these overviews of student learning at least three times a year.

5. Early implementation of research-based interventions
   —This component provides a safety net so that students do not have to "wait to fail" before being provided with extra support that is in addition to the core instructional program.

6. Progress monitoring during intervention
   —Student progress is monitored frequently and instruction is fine-tuned based on this progress, or lack thereof; hence the name, "response to the intervention." When lack of progress is noted, there must be provision of additional instruction at increasing levels of intensity, using interventions that target the identified skill deficit.

7. Fidelity Measures
   —This aspect refers to the level of effectiveness of the instruction/intervention that the teacher provides, more specifically whether the intervention and/or data collection is being implemented as intended and with consistency.

Although there is flexibility to the RTI model, a few basic activities are necessary before an RTI process becomes customary practice in a building. These may include but are not limited to:
- development of a school-wide plan that is spearheaded by administration with support of various stakeholders;
- listing of currently available interventions and supports that are in the school to meet some of the challenges that are presented by struggling learners;
- categorization of those interventions as they relate to the three tiers of the model;
- identification of additional materials and supports that are needed to ensure a solid range of interventions;
- assessment of any existing building level teams, and/or a process to ensure the availability of a problem-solving team that can assist and support the successful implementation of RTI.

To most effectively implement RTI a multi-disciplinary team is necessary and may include: a building administrator, reading teacher, school psychologist, speech therapist, general education teacher and special education teacher. The responsibility of this team is multi-fold but should include no less than:
- reviewing referring teacher's concerns about student academic difficulties and assessing the difference between student performance and that of grade level peers;
- identifying student strengthens as well as interests;
- reviewing baseline data that has been collected;

- designing intervention plans that include projected outcomes and methods for assessing progress;
- determining staff member who will implement the intervention and the length of time it should be in place prior to review;
- monitoring progress based upon the data collected in reference to the specific intervention that is being provided;
- developing a plan to communicate steps of the process with students' parents.

RTI and Learning Disabilities

The 2004 reauthorization of the IDEA included language that allows states to use an RTI process rather than an I.Q. discrepancy model for the identification of students with learning disabilities. This is one of the most positive aspects of the RTI process as it offers an option to the difficulty, failure and/or lack of progress that students have to experience before demonstrating their marked "gap" or discrepancy from other students. It also potentially reduces the number of students who are erroneously identified a having a learning disability when the learning problems are due to cultural/ language differences or lack of adequate instruction.

Almost two years after the reauthorization, the final federal regulations went into effect. They provide that each State:
- *Must not require* the use of severe discrepancy between intellectual ability and achievement for determining whether a child has a specific learning disability;
- *Must permit* the use of a process based on the child's response to scientific, research-based interventions;
- *May permit* the use of other alternative research-based procedures for determining whether a child has specific learning disability.

In addition the federal regulations:
- Establish highly prescriptive procedures for assessing whether a child's underachievement in reading is due to the lack of appropriate reading instruction in general education.

The regulations also stipulate that each State:
- *Must develop* criteria applicable to the federally mandated procedures for determining whether a child has a learning disability as defined by law;
- *Must determine* whether to permit the use of other alternate research-based procedures for determining if a child has a specific learning disability.

As a result of the new regulations, each local school district:
- *May be permitted* to use other alternative research-based procedures if its State authorizes their use;
- *Must use* the State's criteria to establish whether the child achieved adequately, based on age or the State's approved grade level standards;

- *Must decide* whether it will continue to rely on the severe discrepancy model, the RTI model, or both.

Districts and schools throughout the country are beginning to embrace RTI, some slowly, others with more confidence and enthusiasm. As with all initiatives there are reservations on many levels but the bottom line appears to be recognition that RTI is a process that incorporates best practices, solid instruction and sound research. With these as its components, it is positioned to have a meaningful impact on the teaching-learning process.

Positive Behavioral Supports

Positive behavior supports describe the overall efforts of schools to provide a safe and orderly learning environment for all students. This ensures that students with disabilities receive the free appropriate public education (FAPE) to which they are entitled, per IDEA; it also ensures that their non-disabled peers receive the education to which they are entitled.

A summary of Positive Behavioral Intervention and Supports.
- administrative involvement and support are essential in a whole school approach to positive behavior.
- positive behavior support is the application of positive behavioral interventions and systems to achieve positive change.
- positive behavior support is an approach to discipline & intervention that is proving effective and practical in schools.
- positive behavior change is the application of the science of behavior to achieve socially important change, with the focus being on change that is durable, comprehensive, and linked to academic and social gains.
- generally, positive behavior support should be applied before any child is excluded from school due to a problem behavior.
- functional behavioral assessment (FBA) is a systematic way of identifying problem behaviors and the events that predict occurrence, non-occurrence, and maintenance of those behaviors.
- the FBA is the foundation on which positive behavioral support is delivered.
- strong, administrative leadership, support and participation is needed to increase effective efforts.
- positive behavior support considers multiple contexts, including community, family, district, school, classroom, non-classroom, and individual.
- a proactive perspective is maintained along a continuum, using the three tier model wherein Tier I is primary (what we do for all), Tier II is secondary (what we do for some), and Tier III is tertiary (what we do for a few) prevention & interventions.

Some of the most significant benefits of implementing positive behavioral supports are:

- reduction in office discipline referrals;
- improved access of all students to academic engaged time and improved academic performance;
- success rate for interventions based on a prior functional assessment is almost twice that obtained when this type of assessment is not conducted.

How do positive behavior supports relate to the law?
Attention to individual student behavior has always been a concern in special education law, primarily in the development of services for students with severe emotional disturbance (SED). In recent years, as violence has become an issue for the nation's schools, Congress has addressed behavior issues in various pieces of legislation. One of these is in the reauthorized IDEA; therein behavior is identified as one of the special factors that the IEP Team must consider.

In addressing issues of behavior and discipline, there are three primary factors that must be considered. They are:
- IDEA's absolute commitment to provide students with disabilities a free appropriate public education;
- concern that the behavior of students with disabilities neither precludes their education nor substantially interferes with that of class/schoolmates; and
- expectation that the school will design and implement a program that addresses students' needs.

Over the course of almost four decades since the passage of P.L. 94–142, successive revisions of the law and a myriad of court decisions have sought to strike a balance among these three factors. As of the passage of IDEA 2004, these are:
- students with disabilities may not be denied a free appropriate public education, regardless of the behavior. Where the behavior is such as to warrant removal from the classroom (or school) to an alternative educational setting or a penal institution, educational services may not cease. These services must enable the students to progress toward meeting their IEP goals.
- the same disciplinary procedures as applied to non-disabled students may be applied to students with disabilities when the violation of the school/district code of conduct is not a manifestation of the student's disability.
- when the behavior is alleged not to be a manifestation of the students' disability, the school, on a case-by-case basis, may consider any unique circumstances that warrant a change of placement for a violation of the school/district code of conduct. This may include a change of placement, including suspension for up to 10 days.
- within 10 days of a student's change of placement for a violation of the school/district code of conduct, a meeting of the parent(s), representative of the LEA, and members of the IEP Team, must be convened to determine whether the conduct was caused by or had

a direct and substantial relationship to the student's disability or was a result of the failure of the school to implement the student's IEP. This process, called a "manifestation" determination, was placed in the 1997 IDEA amendments.
- if the manifestation determination results in a finding that the conduct was a manifestation of the student's disability or of the failure of the LEA to implement the student's IEP, a Functional Behavioral Assessment (FBA) must be conducted and a Behavioral Intervention Plan (BIP) implemented and incorporated into the IEP. (More information about FBAs and BIPS will be found at the end of this chapter.) During this time students are to be returned to the placement from which they were removed. An exception to this is if the conduct involved weapons, drugs, or serious bodily injury. In such cases, per IDEA 2004, the student may be removed to an alternative education placement for up to 45 school days.

When and for whom are positive behavior supports needed?

The goal of providing a safe learning environment requires positive behavior supports be in place for all students. There has been a charge that the provisions of IDEA hinder school discipline by allowing students with disabilities to use negative behavior that would not be tolerated from nondisabled students. Also, that students with disabilities are not allowed to be punished for the same misbehavior that would lead to punishment for nondisabled students. The thinking of advocates, reflected in IDEA regulations, is that if the misbehavior is a function of the student's disability, then the appropriate response is to change the student's program not punish him or her. In response to such concerns, Congress commissioned a study, conducted by its investigative arm, the U.S. General Accounting Office in 2001. The overall findings of the study were that, "students with disabilities who are involved in violence or other serious incidents at school are being punished in the same way as other students who commit comparable acts ...."[60] The study, based on a survey of middle and high school principals, reported that both students with and without disabilities received suspensions of a similar length, and that both groups were expelled from school or placed in alternative settings at about the same rate, e.g., about one in six of those who engaged in serious misconduct. Principals generally rated their schools special-education-discipline policies, both those under IDEA and local policies, as having a positive or neutral effect on school safety and orderliness.[61] On the other hand, about a fifth of the principals objected to a separate discipline policy for students with disabilities and found the IDEA procedures burdensome and time-consuming.

There is increasing attention in education to addressing the behavioral barriers to learning present in schools, identifying the schools' role in fostering negative behaviors as well as their role in encouraging and supporting students' positive behavior. Among the myriad of terms used are discipline programs, violence prevention, behavior management, and classroom management. In this book, misbehavior will be used to denote the behavior being addressed and positive behavior support will be used to describe the intervention.

Before turning to the approaches used in positive behavior support programs there are some basic factors to keep in mind:
- the IDEA presumption of serving students in the general education environment with the necessary supplementary aids and services.
- the IDEA requirement that schools address the full range of the student's educational needs, social and emotional, as well as academic; just as the student's disability may entail academic consequences requiring special education services to provide FAPE, so, too, the disability may entail social and behavioral consequences requiring special education services to provide FAPE.
- the provisions of IDEA and the obligations of school districts to meet the needs of individual students with disabilities require a coordinated approach among the home environment, the school, and the classroom.
- an overall consistent school approach requires successful classroom practices to:
    - engage the student in the learning activities;
    - focus on the activities of both the child and the teacher;
    - serve to defuse the immediate issue(s);
    - prevent its extension;
    - develop alternative behaviors; and
    - address the consequences for the other students in the class.[62]

There are numerous issues to consider in regard to the assessment of student behavior. The interdisciplinary nature of the IEP Team provides the forum for such consideration and for determining the nature and location of needed services. Some national data provide context for local considerations.
- greater than half of the referrals for special education are based on emotional or behavioral issues that occur when the student is in grades 3 through 6.
- almost three-fourths of such referrals are boys.
- the most common factor identified in these referrals for both boys and girls is poor peer relationships; others include frustration, low achievement, withdrawn behaviors, disruptive behavior, fighting, refusal to work, and short attention span.
- a disproportionate percentage of African-American students are referred for emotional or behavioral issues, are certified with such labels, and are placed in more restrictive settings.

What is a Functional Behavior Assessment (FBA) and what are its components? How does a FBA relate to a Behavioral Intervention Plan (BIP)?

The FBA is a tool to assist professionals in better understanding a student's problem behavior. By providing essential information about a behavior, it becomes the first step in the development of a

BIP. It is based upon the premise that most people act as they do for a specific reason; that is, behavior actually serves a purpose for the individual. Such purpose may be to avoid/escape doing something, or to ensure that something is done; perhaps it is just for attention. It is the outcome of the action that must be explored; it goes beyond the behavior itself or the symptom, to explore the motivation. Once the cause/reason/function of the behavior is identified and understood, it is easier to develop a plan to teach the student more appropriate ways to fill the need.

Through the FBA process, the team identifies problematic behaviors in very concrete terms. It is important that careful attention be paid to the way information is obtained in this stage of the process. Frequently rating scales and interviews are used, but direct observation of the behavior in the natural environment is, perhaps, the most effective method. The identified behavior must be stated in measurable terms so that data can be gathered to facilitate the FBA process. Once the problem behavior has been isolated, then it is necessary to identify the events (antecedents and setting events) that predict the occurrence and/or maintenance of the behavior. This helps define the condition surrounding the behavior. In the most frequently used FBA model, once the predictors are known, the next step is to identify a desired alternate behavior, always recognizing and carefully assessing ways to make the negative behavior unnecessary and less effective. To maximize the value of the process, the entire team, including student and, when possible, parents works together to develop an approach that fosters the acceptable alternative behavior before the final desired behavior is achieved and maintained.

During the early stages of this process it is critical to determine if the behavior is linked to a deficit in a specific skill area that the student either does not have or is uncomfortable in demonstrating. This is an important factor that may link the behavior and the teaching/learning setting. It also gives clues as to what type of external manipulation of the environment may be effective in addressing the behavior.

The most significant step is translating the information gained in the FBA into strategies that will effectively support the change in behavior. This becomes the BIP, a clearly formatted action plan agreed to by all stakeholders. It identifies who is responsible for what aspect of this process. It includes positive strategies, curricular modifications and supplementary aids and supports that are required to address the identified concern. In this way focus is on the need behind the inappropriate behavior, and the intervention is based on the identified cause of this behavior.

Although the FBA and BIP are both concerned with negative or unacceptable behaviors, it is important that they both be carried out within an environment that is strength-based. Not only will this give the students a more comfortable setting but it will also provide teachers with exceptionally valuable information about the effectiveness of their teaching style and classroom management techniques. Because this approach uses the environment of the student as springboard, it invites all members of the team to be involved as they all have potential—though perhaps of differing degree—to exert influence on this environment.

Behavior: Beliefs and Responses

According to Crone (2010) underlying Functional Behavioral Interventions (FBA) and Behavior Intervention Plans (BIP) are a set of basic beliefs about behaviors. These include:
- Behavior serves a purpose or "function";
- Behavior is related to the context where and under what conditions it occurs;
- Behavior is a complex response to a dynamic relationship among many variables: (people, places and events);
- If the positive behaviors expected for students are taught, the amount, frequency, and intensity of problem behavior can be decreased or minimized; and
- If a problem behavior can be defined, explained and predicted, there is a likelihood it can be prevented.

There is a general sequence from behavior to intervention:
- Identifying and defining the problem behavior;
- Gathering information;
- Generating a summary statement, incorporating setting events, antecedents, behaviors, and consequences;
- Developing a behavioral intervention plan;
- Implementing the plan; and
- Assessing, monitoring, and modifying the plan.

School-Wide Systems for Behavioral Supports

In building school-wide systems, the following approaches have been successful:
- a small number of clear behavioral expectations are defined;
- teaching of these behavioral expectations is the role of all staff;
- appropriate behaviors are acknowledged;
- behavioral errors are corrected systematically and proactively;
- administrative support and involvement are ongoing; and
- classroom and individual student support systems are integrated within the school-wide system.

"Unified discipline" is one among many systemwide programs. While particular to that program, the following features can be considered more generally.

Unified attitudes: All participants adopt a consistent point of view about encouraging appropriate behavior and correcting misbehavior. All participants support the belief that all students are able to improve their behavior. All participants provide correction in a professional manner and support the belief that anger and emotional upset undermine instructional effectiveness.

Unified expectations: All participants reach consensus on school rules, classroom rules, and classroom procedures. Unified sets of rules are developed across each grade.

Unified correction: A uniform verbal correction procedure and a consistent set of consequences is developed.

Unified team roles: Support is available for students who are difficult to manage, and clear roles and responsibilities are established for the entire school team.

Classroom Positive Behavior Support Systems

Classwide systems must be developed and implemented aligned with the school-wide system.

The following materials provide guiding questions:
- "Developing Classroom Expectations and Routines: A Self-Study Guide," **Blackline Master No. 12,** page 133.
- "Effective Classroom Management Practices: A Self-Study Guide," **Blackline Master No. 13,** page 134.
- "Approaches of School, Classroom, and Student-Focused Practices: A Self-Study Guide," **Blackline Master No. 14,** page 135.

Measuring the climate of a classroom—that hum of engaged work—is a subtle matter. The Pennsylvania instructional support system suggests four areas of attention at the classroom level and five areas in terms of individual students.

Classroom-based indicators of the need for change:
1. Disruptive behavior. As a general rule, a problem exists if disruptive behaviors occur more than once per hour (or class period) on the average.
2. On-task rates. Problematic if more than 2 or 3 students are off-task at any given time.
3. Completion of assignments. Generally a problem if 10 percent or more of the students often do not complete their work on time.
4. Student cooperation. A problem is if after a few weeks of school students continue to need constant reminders to follow classroom procedures.

Individual student indicators of the need for change:
1. Lack of increases in alternative skills,
2. Lack of reduction in problem behaviors,
3. Lack of maintenance or generalization of alternative skills,
4. Limited lifestyle enhancements,
5. Student and/or family displeasure in impact/outcomes.

Distinguishing the behavior addressed allows for focused interventions. Three broad groupings are non-compliant or deviant behaviors, inattentive behaviors, and hyperactive behaviors. For each there are separate descriptors and response strategies.

What are the roles of administrators, teachers, clinicians, and parents regarding positive behavior supports?
Positive behavior supports for individual students must be embedded in a school-wide program of positive behavior support. The establishment of such a program and the commitment of the necessary resources and follow–through are central activities of school administration. Developing a school-wide plan involves the systematic collection of data and analysis, the development of a consensus-based body of behavioral expectations and consequences (positive and negative), establishment of a school policy (consonant with federal and state law and district policy), allocation of staff resources to develop and implement the system, and support for regular review and revision. Each of these features of a school-wide positive behavior support program will require administrative involvement and support.

Teachers have a key role in gathering information and managing student disruptive behavior. While not ignoring the consequences of the child's disability, it is important for the teacher first to address questions concerning the overall activities of the classroom.

Some examples are as follows:
- Is the instructional program appropriate to meet the student's needs?
- Are needed related services and supplementary aids and services in place?
- Is the student effectively engaged in the learning activities?
- Does the student understand the concepts being taught?
- Does the student have the study skills necessary to learn the material?
- Are there factors of physical arrangement, boredom or frustration that limit the student's learning?
- Does the student know the processes of transition? From one activity to another? From one setting to another?

Extra-school factors, such as issues in the student's home or family life must be considered. In gathering information about the student and circumstances that surround the misbehavior, the following questions may serve as a guide:
- When is the student most likely to engage in problem behaviors?
- What specific events appear to be contributing to the problem situation?
- What function(s) do(es) the problem behavior serve for the student?
- What might the student be communicating?
- When is the student less likely to engage in problem behaviors?

During the FBA/BTP process clinical/support team collaboration is essential. These staff members can be extremely helpful in the observation and data collection phase, as well as during implementation. Due to their specific training and experience, they add a unique dimension to the understanding of the academic, behavioral, and social components of the student.

Parental involvement in developing a positive behavior support program for an individual student is essential. This includes involvement in the conduct of the Functional Behavioral Assessment, the development of the behavior intervention plan, the consideration of "antecedent" events, the development and reinforcement of alternative skills, and the establishment of lifestyle interventions. While home and school are different environments, each can support the other in promoting positive student behavior. Most parents are willing to be involved in creating positive behavior, and may request support in gaining new skills in this area. Indeed, such training is one of the most frequent requests from parents. In conducting such training, parent-to-parent activities are an important resource.

General Consideration for Positive Behavior Supports
In developing a positive behavior support program for individual students, there are a number of factors that are enablers of success and others that may be seen as inhibitors.

Enablers
- A sense of urgency usually surrounds events of serious student misbehavior.
- There is a growing body of successful experience that can be called upon.
- A child-centered focus leads to measurable outcomes.
- Educators can relate to the pedagogic approach of positive behavior support.
- Changes in IDEA promote positive behavior support efforts.
- The failure of punishment and exclusion has been well documented.
- The process provides opportunities for educators and families to collaborate.
- A well-developed support plan can have far-reaching positive outcomes for child, family, and school.

Inhibitors
- The initial point of entry is often in response to crisis.
- The process takes time and may involve a reassignment of resources.
- Often schools are seeking a quick fix.
- Positive behavior support requires a team approach and ongoing commitment from school personnel.
- The exigencies of school life too often preclude the needed follow through.

Underlying all positive behavior support systems are a set of four assumptions:
1. Challenging behaviors are context related. They occur for a reason and are not simply a manifestation of the individual's

disability. When they do occur they likely signal that something in the prevailing environment is disturbing or provoking the individual.
2. Challenging behaviors serve a function for the student. While socially unacceptable, these behaviors enable the student to escape or avoid unpleasant events, gain access to desired activities or social interactions.
3. Effective interventions are based on a thorough understanding of the person, his or her social contexts, and the function of the problem behavior.
4. Positive behavior support must be grounded in person-centered values that respect the dignity, preferences, and goals of each student.[63]

The following table of "Misbehavior Messages" may serve as a guide in understanding the function and the possible meaning of the misbehavior.

Misbehavior Messages

Function	*Possible messages*
To gain access to social interaction	"Play with me."
	"Watch what I am doing."
	"Did I do good work?"
	"Spend time with me."
	"Let's do this together."
	"Can I have a turn, too?"
	"I want to be one of the group."
To gain access to activities, objects.	"I want to play outside."
	"Can I have what s/he has?"
	"I don't want to stop this."
	"I'm hungry."
To terminate/avoid unwanted situations	"Leave me alone."
	"This is too hard."
	"I need help."
	"I don't want to do this."
	"Don't tell me what to do."
	"I don't like to be teased."
	"I'm bored."
	"I'm not feeling well."
	"I need a break."
To gain access to stimulating events	"I like doing this."[64]

In recent years, student discipline programs have shifted from a sole focus on an individual student with a "problem" behavior to the need for school-wide behavior support systems. Instead of a patchwork of individual behavior management plans, schools are moving toward a systemic approach that addresses the classroom, areas outside of the classroom, and the individual student.

The next table provides a guide of "Proactive Strategies" to minimize misbehavior.

Proactive strategies

Strategy	Instructional example	Social example
Remove a problem event	Avoid giving difficult word problems for independent seatwork Avoid requiring repetitive tasks	Avoid crowded settings Avoid long delays
Modify a problem event	Shorten lessons Reduce the number of problems on a page Modify instruction to decrease errors Increase lesson pace	Change voice intonation Modify a boring schedule Use suggestive rather than directive language
Intersperse difficult or unpleasant events with easy or pleasant events	Mix difficult problems with easier ones Mix mastered tasks with acquisition Tasks for seatwork	Schedule nonpreferred activities with preferred ones Precede directives for non-preferred activities with easily followed directions
Add events that promote desired behaviors	Provide choice of tasks, materials, activities Include student preferences Use cooperative learning strategies to encourage participation State clear expectations at start of lesson	Schedule preferred activities in daily routines Provide a variety of activities Provide opportunities for social interactions Provide opportunities for physical movement
Block or neutralize the impact of negative events	Offer frequent breaks Reduce demands when student upset	Provide opportunities for rest Provide time alone Provide time to regroup after negative experience[64]

In January of 2001, an email message was sent to all school superintendents by Judith E. Heumann, Assistant Secretary, Office of Special Education and Rehabilitative Services, and Kenneth Warlick, Director, Office of Special Education Programs, US Department of Education. Excerpts from that message provide an excellent summary that remains relevant today.

Prevention Research & the IDEA Discipline Provisions: A Guide for School Administrators

An Ounce of Prevention

The Challenge: Creating, Safe, Effective, and Orderly Learning Environments

- To be effective learning environments, schools need to be safe and orderly.
- Problem behavior is the single most common reason why students are referred for removal from school.
- Challenges facing educators are significant and persistent.
- Across the nation schools are being asked to do more with less.
- Punishment and exclusion remain the most common responses to problem behavior by students.
- Reprimands, detention, and exclusion are documented as ineffective strategies for improving the behavior of students.

Impact of the Challenge: How Negative Behavior Impacts Schools

- Loss of instructional time for all students
- Exclusion of students
- Time away from teaching and learning
- Overemphasis on reactive discipline & classroom management practices to control behavior
- Chaotic school environments that disenfranchise families & school staff
- Ineffective & inefficient use of student and staff resources & time

A Systematic Solution: Creating School Wide Responses

Creating of host environments that support preferred & effective practices, and include:

- policies (proactive discipline handbooks, procedural handbooks)
- structures (behavior support teams)
- routines (opportunities for students to learn expected behavior, staff development, data-based decision-making)
- schools successful in dealing with behavior realize that all children need behavior support. They define, teach, monitor, and acknowledge appropriate social behavior for all students. They do not wait for students to fail before providing behavior supports.
- establishment of proactive environments that have the capacity to identify, adapt, and sustain effective policies, systems, and research validated practices.
- focus attention on creating and sustaining school environments that improve results for all children by making problem behavior less effective, efficient, and relevant; and desired behavior more functional.

Where can I find additional information about interventions, response to intervention and positive behavior supports?

Overall information is available from The Center on Positive Behavioral Intervention and Supports, 5262 University of Oregon, Eugene, OR 97403–5262, (541) 346–2505. Their Web Site is at www.pbis.org. Information on school safety and violence prevention is available from the Center for Effective Collaboration and Practice, 1000 Thomas Jefferson Street, NW, Washington, DC 20007 (888) 457-1551. Their Web Site is at www.air.org/cecp.

In the past several years, many state education departments have developed material in this area. Notable has been the work in Pennsylvania and Michigan. See esp.,

Bateman, Barbara D. & Annemieke Golly. *Why Johnny Doesn't Behave: Twenty Tips for Measurable BIPs*. Verona, WI: Attainment Company, Inc., 2003.

Boynton, Mark & Christine Boynton. *The Educator's Guide to Preventing & Solving Discipline Problems*. Alexandria, VA: Association for Supervision and Curriculum Development, 2005.

Connor, Daniel F. *Aggression and Antisocial Behavior in Children and Adolescents: Research and Treatment*. New York, NY: The Guilford Press, 2004.

Crawford, Glenda B. *Managing the Adolescent Classroom*. Thousand Oaks, CA: Corwin Press, 2004.

Crone, Deanne A. & Robert H. Horner. *Building Positive Behavior Support Systems in Schools: Functional Behavioral Assessment*. New York, NY: Guilford Press, 2003.

Crone, D.A., Hawken, L.S., and Horner, R.H. *Responding to Problem Behavior in Schools, 2nd Ed*. New York, NY:Guilford Press, 2010.

Ditrano, C. *FBA and BIP* (laminated reference guide). Port Chester, NY: Dude Publishing, 2010.

Fad, Kathleen McConnell & James R. Patton. *Behavioral Intervention Planning*. Austin, TX: Pro-Ed, Inc., 2000.

Halvorsen, A .T. and Neary, T. *Building Inclusive Schools: Tools and Strategies for Success*. Upper Saddle River, NJ, Pearson, 2009.

Janney, Rachel & Martha E. Snell. *Behavioral Support: Teachers' Guides to Inclusive Practices*. Baltimore, MD: Paul H. Brookes Publishing Co., Inc., 2000.

Kemp, Karen A. & Mary Ann Eaton. *RTI: The Classroom Connection for Literacy*. Port Chester, NY: National Professional Resources, Inc. 2008.

Mather, Nancy & Sam Goldstein. *Learning Disabilities and Challenging Behaviors: A Guide to Intervention and Classroom Management.* Baltimore, MD: Brookes Publishing Company, 2001.

Nelsen, Jane, Lynn Lott & H. Stephen Glenn. Positive Discipline In The Classroom: Developing Mutual Respect, Cooperation, and Responsibility in Your Classroom. Three Rivers, MI: Three Rivers Press, 2000.

Norlander, Karen (featured presenter). RTI Tacakles the LD Explosion: A Good IDEA Becomes Law (DVD). National Profesional Resoureces, Inc. 2007

Reider, Barbara. Teach More and Discipline Less. Thousand Oaks, CA: Corwin Press, 2005.

Shore, Kenneth. The ABCs of Bullying Prevention. Port Chester, NY: Dude Publishing, 2005.

Watson, T. Steuart & Mark W. Steege. Conducting School-Based Functional Behavioral Assessments: A Practitioner's Guide. New York, NY: Guilford Press, 2003.

Wood, M. Mary & Nicholas Long. Life Space Intervention: Talking with Children and Youth in Crisis Austin, TX: Pro-Ed, Inc., 1991.

Wright, Jim. RTI Toolkit: A Practical Guide for School. National Professional Resources, Inc. 2008.

Wunderlich, Kathy C. The Teacher's Guide to Behavioral Interventions. Columbia, MO: Hawthorne Educational Services, Inc., 1988.

BLM No. 12

DEVELOPING CLASSROOM EXPECTATIONS AND ROUTINES: A SELF-STUDY GUIDE

Effective instructional activities can engage students, and, as a consequence, make misbehavior less likely.

- Am I teaching useful, appropriate, and important knowledge and skills to the students?

- Am I using effective instructional strategies and curricula to teach these skills and knowledge?

- Have I taught classroom rules and expectations directly to the students?

- Have students demonstrated mastery of classroom expectations and routines?

- What obstacles prevent students from performing desired classroom expectations and routines?

- Have I taught and do I use procedures for encouraging appropriate displays of classroom rules and expectations?

- Have I taught and do I use a continuum of procedures for discouraging/preventing rule violation?

- Do I modify my instruction to maximize student learning and to accommodate individual student differences?

- Do I have procedures in place for monitoring student behavior and the effectiveness of my classroom management practices?

Inclusion: A Service, Not A Place, by Dorothy Kerzner Lipsky and Alan Gartner

EFFECTIVE CLASSROOM MANAGEMENT PRACTICES: A SELF-STUDY GUIDE

While not every classroom problem can be anticipated, there is empirical evidence of effective classroom practices. Teachers using such practices can often preclude problems. The following questions can serve as a guide.

- Do I provide advance organizers or pre-corrections?

These function as reminders of expected behaviors before students enter into a situation where problem behaviors many be manifested. For example, before students are to move to the next activity, the teacher says," Be sure you collect all your materials, put your completed papers on my desk, and line up."

- Are students kept engaged?

To engage students, the instructional activity must maintain their attention, positive reinforcement provided, and access to positive reinforcement for other activities minimized.

- Is a positive focus provided?

The activity must be presented in a positive light, more positive than negative interactions provided, problem behaviors anticipated and cut short.

- Are classroom rules consistently enforced?

Rules for all students must be consistent.

- Are rule violations and social behavior errors corrected proactively?

In the context of a previously established rule, error correction should be routine and not divert from the lesson itself.

- Do I plan smooth transitions?

It is important to alert students to the transition, inform them of the expected behavior, follow routines consistently, and provide regular feedback to students.

Inclusion: A Service, Not A Place, by Dorothy Kerzner Lipsky and Alan Gartner

BLM No. 14

APPROACHES OF SCHOOL, CLASSROOM, AND STUDENT-FOCUSED PRACTICES: A SELF-STUDY GUIDE

When (mis)behavior by a student requires attention, there is a combination of schoolwide policy, classroom procedures, and individual attention that must be considered. The following approaches can help a teacher to manage or forestall (mis)behavior. The approaches can serve as guiding questions for teachers to consider in their classroom practices.

In my classroom, do I:

- apply schoolwide rules,

_____

- explicitly teach schoolwide and class rules expectations/rules,

_____

- model and have students role play "problem" situations,

_____

- teach social skills and skills of self-management,

_____

- support students' setting personal goals,

_____

- teach students self-monitoring goals and encourage their use,

_____

- use positive correction prompts,

_____

- establish a clear set of consequences, positive and negative, for (mis)behavior,

_____

- build opportunities for movement within a lesson,

_____

- provide a structure ("scaffold") for the learning activity,

_____

- establish alternative work areas,

_____

- proactively decrease distractions and reduce unstructured activities,

_____

- provide active learning opportunities for student participation,

_____

- provide reminders/cues for appropriate behavior, and

_____

- explain the purposes and expectations for each activity?

_____

Inclusion: A Service, Not A Place, by Dorothy Kerzner Lipsky and Alan Gartner

8
Technology, Assistive Technology, and Universal Design for Learning

Technology in schools covers a wide gamut of devices and techniques, from a special grip on a pencil to a machine that provides oral presentation of print text, from simple devices to highly sophisticated systems. Greater demands in learning activities, as well as concerns that students be well equipped to enter the workforce, have led to an extraordinary expansion in the use of technology, especially computers, both for non-disabled students and for those with disabilities.[66] That students are coming to school more comfortable and skilled in the age of the Internet is both challenge and opportunity for the schools.

In addition to the computer, which is clearly the most commonly used technology, there are many simple low-tech, less expensive solutions that can be used to assist students. These can be related to positioning, environmental control, mobility, self-care and even recreation. As technology's goal is to compensate for a deficit, its uses are limited only by creativity and integrity!

The introduction of the iPad™ in early 2010 has the potential to be transformational in the education of students with disabilities. (Friedlander and Beske, 2010) As teachers take advantage of its wide range of apps (already well over one hundred thousand) the iPad is not only a tool for overall accessibility, but it also supports inclusion, enabling students with disabilities to participate and learn in integrated settings.

What are "best practices" in the use of technology?
Formal and informal measures indicate that technology, especially the use of computers, can be used to improve what children learn and how they learn, both within school and outside it. But the mere presence of computers, or other technological tools, does not ensure their effective use. For this to occur, technology must enhance fundamental principles of learning, including active engagement of the student, participation in groups, frequent interaction and feedback, and connections to real-world contexts.[67]

The use of technology as an effective learning tool is more likely to take place when it is embedded in the broad educational activities of the classroom, rather than as an activity separate and apart from the overall instructional program as represented by the separate computer laboratory. More specifically, students trained in collaborative learning on computers in small groups had higher achievement, better self-esteem, and more positive attitudes toward learning than students working individually. Such results, according to Sivin-Kachala and Bialo (2001), were particularly pronounced for low-ability students. Students who worked in groups were found to interact more with other students, to use more appropriate learning strategies, and to persevere more on assigned instructional tasks.

Too often in the past, and especially for students with significant disabilities, the "magic" of the technology held it apart from the overall program of instruction and separated disabled students from their nondisabled peers. Increasingly, however, technology (including assistive technology) is being seen as a "diversity accommodation tool,"[68] essential to promoting IEP goals regarding inclusion, by providing access to the curriculum, peer-to-peer communication, and alternative ways to assess progress. Computers are powerful tools that can provide multi-sensory information in ways that captivate and motivate students involved in the learning process. Computers and computer-based devices can also provide easier access to text and alternate ways to write, speak, see, listen, calculate, move, and experience the world.

Some pedagogically sound, general principles that apply to the use of technology and promote inclusive practices follow:

Principles in the Use of Technology
- Select programs and software with built-in cooperative features.
- Develop peer support (or "buddy") programs that involve classmates helping classmates. While traditionally these efforts have involved non-disabled students assisting those with disabilities, as discussed in Chapter 6, students with disabilities can play the role of helper as well.
- Ensure that the technology program for students with disabilities meshes with the school's overall technology plan. This does not mean ignoring IEP-determined assistive technology needs of students with disabilities. Rather, it ensures that those resources are incorporated within the overall school and classroom. (With the reauthorized IDEA revoking the "incidental benefits" rule, services and equipment for students with disabilities may also benefit nondisabled students.)
- Incorporate the use of technology as an integral part of the instructional program. Unless teachers are prepared to do this, educational technology will not fulfill its promise. The lack of appropriate technology training in pre-service and in-service teacher education programs is the most commonly cited barrier to the effective use of technology in the classroom.

- Focus on professional development utilizing the collaboration between general and special education teachers, embedding use of technology in the actual teaming of the classroom.
- Provide support for teachers in selecting, operating and maintaining the equipment, as well as infusing the use of technology into the curriculum.
- Clarify expectations at the same time as support is provided; the effective use of technology is an essential part of a quality instructional program, i.e., it is non-negotiable.
- The use of technology should not be limited to only selected subjects, activities or students.

There are a myriad of technology uses, ranging from high to low tech, across the full range of the curriculum. These include:
- cooperative learning programs (see esp. the "Learning Together" models of Johnson and Johnson);
- texts available in various formats;
- multi-media formats to augment print presentation, as well as those with options for transformation from one medium to another (e.g., text-to-speech);
- Universal Design for Learning (UDL) material that provides presentations at multiple levels of design, complexity, and format;
- word processing programs that support proper spelling, grammar, and organization;
- spreadsheets and other programs for calculations;
- tape recordings of lessons;
- books on tape;
- computer software that converts printed text into Braille or voice;
- computers that have expanded keyboards and/or are switch or voice activated;
- enlarged print and/or electronic enlargement devices;
- linkages to the Internet to acquire information, "visit" distant sites, communicate with persons at a distance;
- computer software that enables teachers to assess a student's mastery of material and to design appropriate instructional and curricular modifications;
- computer software, matched to learning styles, that enables students to master curricular goals, in a manner paced to their rhythm;
- touch screens;
- optical character recognition technology that can scan and read text aloud;
- classroom amplification and voice enhancement systems; and
- varied social media systems.

Federal legislation in August of 2006 mandated that all textbook publishers of K-12 materials make print instructional materials available in the National Instructional Materials Accessibility Stand

(NIMAS) format. This is intended to help ensure that students with "print disabilities" have efficient and timely access to instructional materials.

What is assistive technology (AT)? How does it relate to the law?
As technology has taken hold in every other aspect of our economy and in daily life, its impact has been and will continue to be monumental in education.

AT enables the user to be more self-confident, independent and more fully integrated into the classroom. Assistive Technology is defined in the law as "any item, piece of equipment, or product system... that is used to increase, maintain, or improve functional capabilities of children with disabilities." Furthermore, an assistive technology service is defined as "any service that directly assists an individual with a disability in the selection, acquisition, or use of an assistive technology device." As with all IDEA services, assistive technology is to be provided for the child without cost to her/him or the family. Services may include:
- evaluation of the needs of the individual with a disability;
- provision of assistive technology devices;
- coordination of technology use with other interventions; and
- training and/or technical assistance to the individual with disabilities, to professionals who work with the individual, and to family members in the use of the device(s).

When first appearing on the educational scene, assistive technology was considered primarily for use with students whose disabilities were more severe. However, as more educators have become knowledgeable in the field and aware of the tremendous advantages offered through assistive technology solutions, students with less serious disabilities as well as students in the general education population have become beneficiaries. For all students the goal is increased independence, greater participation, and enhanced performance. A unified approach enhances the likelihood of broader training across all staff and provides for more resource sharing across budgets.

Assistive technology has tremendous potential and value in supporting the goal of schools in providing high quality, accessible education to all students. Perhaps one of the major thrusts in education in the first years of the twenty-first century has been differentiated instruction. Clearly assistive technology is an excellent resource for every teacher who seeks to truly differentiate.

The challenge for many districts is the assignment of staff and allocation of dollars to meet these mandates. It is also providing the training necessary to ensure that the IEP team is sufficiently knowledgeable to discharge its responsibility. This means they must know the nuances of the student's disability in relationship to the uniqueness of the various Assistive Technology solutions.

In *Assistive Technology: What Every Educator Needs to Know,* Brian Friedlander (2010) outlines the many tools to support students both disabled and non-disabled. These include:

- Alternates to the Keyboard
    — Hardware Solutions
        - Alternative keyboards
        - Touch screens
        - Switch access
    — Software Solutions
        - On-Screen Keyboards
        - Speech Recognition
- Mouse Alternatives
    — Trackball
    — Trackpad
    — Joystick
    — MouseKeys
- Communication Tools
    — Communication board
        - Boardmaker
    — Output communication aides
        - GoTalks
        - BigMacs
        - MessageMates
        - Picture It
- Writing Tools
    — Portable notetakers
    — Netbooks
    — Talking word processors
    — Word Prediction software
    — Spelling tools
- Reading Tools
    — Text Scanners
    — Audio/Digital Books
    — Screen Readers
- Multimedia Tools
    — Powerpoint
    — IMovie
    — Hyperstudio
    — Pixie 2

What is Universal Design for Learning (UDL)?

One of the significant challenges for educators is the issue of accessibility, for both disabled and non-disabled students. The challenge is to both the student and the system. Too often in education focus is on the student limits. Too often the failures of the system are not recognized. This is reminiscent of the realities of a half century ago. Then, persons with disabilities were denied access to many buildings and other facilities, not by law but design—e.g., entrances with stairs, doors not wide enough, restrooms that could not accommodate their needs.

What happened to transform the public environment to enable persons with physical disabilities to have access? The movement in architecture is known as universal design; it recognizes there must be multiple approaches to meet the needs of the diverse public.

Once the 1997 reauthorization of Individuals with Disabilities Education Act set a standard of inclusion of all students in general education, a more daunting question arose in regard to the accessibility of the curriculum. The Universal Design for Learning provides guidance so teachers can respond to the unique and individual needs of ALL their students—this is not only for the special education population, but for non-classified students who have special learning styles or needs, as well as English Language Learners and students who appear to lack motivation or interest. The premise is that features which help those with disabilities will also help others, providing accommodations for the widest array of needs.

The concept of UDL was reinforced by the No Child Left Behind Act which imposed an expectation for improved student performance for all students. The newly reauthorized IDEA re-emphasized this need to present universally designed curriculum to better meet the needs of students with disabilities.

The actual definition of the term emanates from the Assistive Technology Act of 1998: The term 'universal design' means a concept or philosophy for designing and delivering products and services that are usable by people with the widest possible range of functional capabilities, which include products and services that are directly usable (without requiring assistive technologies) and products and services that are made usable with assistive technologies. (U.S.C. § 3002)

The Center for Applied Special Technology (CAST) has addressed the implications of neuroscientific research and, as a result, has identified three primary brain networks, each of which has a unique role in learning. They are the basis of UDL and include:

- Recognition networks which relate to how facts are gathered, and how what is seen, heard, and read is identified and classified; this is referred to as the "what" of learning; they provide multiple means of representation to enable learners various ways of obtaining knowledge and information;
- Strategic networks which relate to planning and performing tasks; how ideas are organized and expressed; this is referred to as the "how" of learning; these networks provide multiple ways of expression and specifically alternatives for demonstrating what is known;
- Affective networks which relate to student engagement; this is referred to as the "why" of learning; these networks provide multiple means of engagement so that students can be motivated based upon their interests.

Through UDL, educators can "differentiate" their teaching to account for these new findings in neuroscience and acknowledge the tremendous diversity in their classrooms. The key factor in UDL solutions is flexibility.

The mandates for inclusion and UDL have become more central to the way schools meet their objectives of positive educational outcomes for all students. These mandates are both charged with the need to address high level curriculum standards through the customization (often referred to by special educators as "modifications and accommodations") of teaching. Again, it is important to note the potential role and significance of these with the Common Core State Standards.

What is the relationship between Assistive Technology (AT) and Universal Design for Learning (UDL)?

Assistive Technology is to the student as UDL is to the curriculum. AT solutions generally address the disability area of targeted student and provide better access for that student or any other student who might benefit from the specific technology. UDL is more of a precursor to the teaching environment, requiring teachers to develop their classrooms and lessons with understanding of the full needs of the student. The availability of multiple UDL methodologies will enhance the efforts of teachers and students to improve student performance. The long term goal is reciprocal: for AT and UDL to become mutually supportive.

A resource for teachers and others who want to learn more about UDL is the "Teaching Every Student (TES)" section of the CAST web site (www.CAST.org, click on "Learning Tools"). The site includes basic ideas and information about UDL and offers toolkits and model lessons. It is presented in a practical manner. An additional resource is the Trace Center at the University of Wisconsin-Madison. It focuses on increasing access to computers and information technologies for people with disabilities and includes a section, "Designing a More Usable World," which employs universal design features It is located at www.Trace.WISC.edu.

Over the course of recent years, there has been sustained questioning in the education arena related to the "average" or "regular" student getting lost. The accusation has often been that so much attention is paid the special populations—those with disabilities, second language learners, the gifted—that the rest of the student body is neglected. Certainly a valid counter to this contention is UDL. It is known that even "average" students have uniqueness in strengths, skills and needs. So the availability of multiple methodologies of UDL will undoubtedly serve them well and assist them in their quest for improved academic performance.

Where can I find additional information regarding technology?
There is an ever-growing body of information about technology, in general, and assistive technology, in particular. Useful resources include:

Children and computer technology (Fall/Winter 2000), *The Future of Children*, 10 (2).

Gordon, D., (Ed.) (2000). *The digital classroom: How technology is changing the way we teach and learn.* Cambridge, MA: The Harvard Education Letter.

The school administrator's Handbook of essential Internet sites. (2000). Gaithersberg, MD: Aspen Publishers.

Sivin-Kachala, J. and Bialo, E.R. (2001). *2000 research report on the effectiveness of technology in schools.* (2001). Washington, DC: Software and Information Industry Association.

Teachers' tools for the 21st century: A report on teachers' use of technology. (2000). Washington, DC: US Department of Education.

More specific resources include the following:

Dean, Stacy P. (2007). *Lesson Plan Book for the Diverse Classroom: Planning for Accessibility through Universal Design for Learning (UDL).* Port Chester, NY: National Professional Resources, Inc.

Elias, Maurice, Friedlander, Brian and Tobias, Steven (2001). *Engaging the Resistant Child Through Computers: A Manual to Facilitate Social and Emotional Learning*, Port Chester, NY: National Professional Resources, Inc.

Edyburn, Dave and Higgins, K. and Boone, Randall. (2005). Handbook of Special Education Technology Research and Practice. Whitefish Bay, WI: Knowledge By Designs, Inc.

Friedlander, Brian (presenter). *Assistive Technology* (DVD). Port Chester, NY: National Professional Resources, Inc. (2009).

Friedlander, B.S. *Assistive Technology: What Every Educator Needs to Know*, (laminated reference guide). Port Chester, NY: Dude Publishing, 2010.

Friedlander, B.S. *Instructional Technology for 21st Century Skills* (laminated reference guide). Port Chester, NY: Dude Publishing, 2010.

Friedlander, B.S. *iPad™: Enhancing Learning and Communication for Students with Special Needs* (laminated reference guide). Port Chester, NY: Dude Publishing, 2012.

Hasselbring, T. S. and Glaser, C. H. W. (Fall/Winter 2000), Use of computer technology to help students with special needs, *The Future of Children*, 10(2), 102–122.

Male, M. (1998). *Technology for inclusion: Meeting the special needs of all students.*, 3rd edition. Boston: Allyn and Bacon.

Pressman, H. and Blackstone, S. (1997). Technology and inclusion: Are we asking the wrong questions? In D.K. Lipsky and A. Gartner, *Inclusion and school reform: Transforming America's classrooms* (pp. 329–352). Baltimore: Paul H. Brookes Publishing Co.

Pressman, H. and Dublin, P. (1994). *Integrating computers in your classroom.* New York: HarperCollins.

Rose, D. H. Meyer, A. (2002). *Teaching Every Student in the Dxxxx Age.* Universal Design for Learning. Alexandria, VA: Association for Supervision and Curriculum Development.

Rose, David H.; Meyer, Anne; Hitchcock, Chuck (2005). *Universally Designed Classroom: Accessible Curriculum and Digital Technologies.* Cambridge, MA: The Harvard Education Press.

9
Additional Resources: Print and Video Materials

**Available from National Professional Resources, Inc.
1–800 453–7461 • www.NPRinc.com**

Allington, Richard L. & Patricia M. Cunningham. *Schools That Work: Where all Children Read and Write.* New York, NY: Harper Collins, 1996.

Anderson, Winifred, Stephen Chitwood, & Diedre Hayden. *Negotiating the Special Education Maze: A Guide for Parents & Teachers.* Bethesda, MD: Woodbine House, 1997.

Armstrong, Thomas. *Beyond the ADD Myth: Classroom Strategies & Techniques* (Video). Port Chester, NY: National Professional Resources, Inc, 1996.

Bateman, Barbara D. & Annemieke Golly. *Why Johnny Doesn't Behave: Twenty Tips for Measurable BIPs.* Verona, WI: Attainment Company, Inc., 2003.

Bateman, Barbara D. & Cynthia M. Herr. *Writing Measurable IEP Goals and Objectives.* Verona, WI: Attainment Company, Inc., 2003.

Batshaw, Mark L. *Children with Disabilities, 5th Edition.* Baltimore, MD: Paul H. Brookes Publishing, 2002.

Bauer, Anne & Glenda Brown. *Adolescents and Inclusion: Transforming Secondary Schools.* Baltimore, MD: Brookes Publishing Company, 2001.

Bender, William. *Differentiating Instruction for Students with Learning Disabilities.* Thousand Oaks, CA: Corwin Press, 2002.

Brady, Kathryn, Mary Beth Forton, Deborah Porter, & Chip Wood. *Rules in School.* Turners Falls, MA: Northeast Foundation for Children, 2003.

Bray, Marty & Abbie Brown, et al. *Technology and the Diverse Learner.* Thousand Oaks, CA: Corwin Press, 2004.

Broun, Leslie & Patricia Oelwein. *Literacy Skill Development for Students with Special Learning Needs: A Strength-Based Approach.* Port Chester, NY: Dude Publishing, 2007.

Buehler, Bruce. *What We Know . . . How We Teach—Linking Medicine & Education for the Child with Special Needs* (Video). Port Chester, NY: National Professional Resources, Inc., 1998.

Burrello, Leonard, Carol Lashly, & Edith E. Beaty. *Educating All Students Together: How School Leaders Create Unified Systems.* Thousand Oaks, CA: Corwin Press, Inc., 2001.

Casbarro, Joseph. *Test Anxiety & What You Can Do About It: A Practical Guide for Teachers, Parents, & Kids.* Port Chester, NY: Dude Publishing, 2005.

Chapman, Carolyn & Rita King. *Differentiated Instructional Strategies for Reading in the Content Areas.* Thousand Oaks, CA: Corwin Press, 2003.

Cohen, Jonathan. *Educating Minds and Hearts: Social Emotional Learning and the Passage into Adolescence.* New York, NY: Teachers College Press, 1999.

Connor, Daniel F. *Aggression and Antisocial Behavior in Children and Adolescents: Research and Treatment.* New York, NY: The Guilford Press, 2004.

Courtae-Little, Ginevra, & Diane M. Browder. *Aligning IEPs to Academic Standards: For Students with Moderate and Severe Disabilities.* Verona, WI: Attainment Company, Inc., 2005.

Crawford, Glenda B. *Managing the Adolescent Classroom.* Thousand Oaks, CA: Corwin Press, 2004.

Crone, Deanne A. & Robert H. Horner. *Building Positive Behavior Support Systems in Schools: Functional Behavioral Assessment.* New York, NY: Guilford Press, 2003.

Crone, D.A., Hawken, L.S., and Horner, R.H. *Responding to Problem Behavior in Schools, 2nd Ed.* New York, NY:Guilford Press, 2010.

Darling-Hammond, Linda. *The New Teacher: Meeting the Challenges* (Video). Port Chester, NY: National Professional Resources, Inc., 2000.

Dean, Stacy P. *Lesson Plan Book for the Diverse Classroom: Planning for Accessibility through Universal Design for Learning.* Port Chester, NY: Dude Publishing, 2007.

Deiner, Penny Low. *Resources for Educating Children with Diverse Abilities, 4th Edition.* Florence, KY: Thomson Delmar Learning, 2004.

Deshler, Donald D. & Jean B. Schumaker. *Teaching Adolescents With Disabilities: Accessing the General Education Curriculum.* Thousand Oaks, CA: Corwin Press, 2005.

Dieker, Lisa. *7 Effective Strategies for Secondary Inclusion (Video).* Port Chester, NY: National Professional Resources, Inc., 2006.

Dieker, L. Hines, R. *Co-Teaching in Secondary Schools: 7 Steps to Successful Inclusion* (laminated referenct guide). Port Chester, NY: Dude Publishing, 2011.

Dieker, Lisa. *Co-Teaching Lesson Plan Book.* Whitefish Bay, WI: Knowledge By Design, 2000.

Dieker, Lisa. *Demystifying Secondary Inclusion: Powerful Strategies (DVD).* Port Chester, NY: National Professional Resources, Inc., 2006.

Ditrano, C. *FBA and BIP* (laminated reference guide). Port Chester, NY: Dude Publishing, 2010.

Dover, Wendy. *The Personal Planner & Training Guide for the Para Professional* (3-ring binder). Manhattan, KS: MASTER Teacher, 1996.

Downing, June and Snell, Martha E. *Including Students with Severe and Multiple Disabilities in Typical Classrooms.* San Francisco, CA: Paul H. Brookes Publishing Co., 2008.

Downing, June E. *Including Students with Severe and Multiple Disabilities in Typical Classrooms, 2nd Edition.* Baltimore, MD: Paul H. Brookes Publishing, 2001.

Elias, Maurice & Linda B. Butler. *Social Decision Making/Social Problem Solving A Curriculum for Academic, Social and Emotional Learning.* Champaign, IL: Research Press, 2005.

Elias, Maurice, Brian Friedlander & Steven Tobias. *Engaging the Resistant Child Through Computers: A Manual to Facilitate Social & Emotional Learning.* Port Chester, NY: Dude Publishing, 2001.

Elias, Maurice & Harriett Arnold. *The Educator's Guide to Emotional Intelligence and Academic Achievement.* Thousand Oaks, CA: Corwin Press, 2006.

Elias, Maurice & Joseph E. Zins, et al. *Promoting Social & Emotional Learning Guidelines for Educators.* Alexandria, VA: ASCD, 1997.

Elliott, Judy L. & Martha L. Thurlow. *Improving Test Performance of Students with Disabilities . . . On District and State Assessments.* Thousand Oaks, CA: Corwin Press, 2000.

Fad, Kathleen McConnell & James R. Patton. *Behavioral Intervention Planning.* Austin, TX: Pro-Ed, Inc., 2000.

Fisher, Douglas, Caren Sax & Ian Pumpian. *Inclusive High Schools.* Baltimore, MD: Paul H. Brookes Publishing, 1999.

Flick, Grad L. *ADD/ADHD Behavior-Change Resource Kit.* West Nyack, NY: Center for Applied Research in Education, 1998.

French, N.K. *A Guide to the Supervision of Paraprofessionals* (laminated reference guide). Port Chester, NY: Dude Publishing, 2008.

Friedlander, Brian. *Assistive Technology* (DVD). Port Chester, NY: National Professional Resources, Inc. (2009).

Friedlander, B.S. *Instructional Technology for 21st Century Skills* (laminated reference guide). Port Chester, NY: Dude Publishing, 2010.

Friedlander, B.S. *iPad™: Enhancing Learning and Communication for Students with Special Needs* (laminated reference guide). Port Chester, NY: Dude Publishing, 2012.

Friend, M. *Co-Teach!* Greensboro, NC: Marilyn French, Inc., 2011.

Friend, Marilyn. *Complexities of Collaboration* (Video). Bloomington, IN: Forum on Education, 2000.

Friend, Marilyn. *The Power of Two: Making a Difference Through Co-Teaching, 2nd Edition* (Video). Bloomington, IN: Forum on Education, 2004.

Friend, Marilyn. *Successful High School Inclusion: Making Access a Reality for All Students* (Video). Bloomington, IN: Forum on Education, 2001.

Friend, Marilyn & Lynne Cooke. *Interactions: Collaboration Skills for School Professionals, 4th Edition.* Boston, MA: Allyn & Bacon, 2002.

Forum on Education (Producer). *Adapting Curriculum & Instruction in Inclusive Classrooms* (Video). Bloomington, IN: 1999.

Fuchs, D., Fuchs, L.S., and Vaughn, S. (Eds.) *Response to Intervention: A Framework for Educators.* Newark, DE: International Reading Association, 2008.

Gardner, Howard. *How Are Kids Smart?* (Video) Port Chester, NY: National Professional Resources, Inc., 1996.

Gardner, Howard. *The Disciplined Mind: What All Students Should Understand.* New York, NY: Simon & Schuster, 1999.

Giangreco, Michael F. *Quick-Guides to Inclusion: Ideas for Educating Students with Disabilities.* Baltimore, MD: Paul H. Brookes Publishing, 1997.

Giangreco, Michael F. *Quick-Guides to Inclusion 2.* Baltimore, MD: Paul H. Brookes Publishing, 1998.

Giangreco, Michael F. *Quick Guides To Inclusion 3: Ideas for Educating Students with Disabilities.* Baltimore, MD: Brookes Publishing Company, 2002.

Giangreco, Michael, Chigee J. Cloninger & Virginia Salce Iverson. *Choosing Outcomes & Accommodations for Children (COACH), 2nd Edition.* Baltimore, MD: Paul H. Brookes Publishing, 1998.

Glass, K.T. *Lesson Design for Differentiated Instruction, Grades 4-9.* Thousand Oaks, CA: Corwin Press, 2009.

Glasser, William. *Choice Theory: A New Psychology of Personal Freedom.* New York, NY: HarperCollins, 1998.

Gold, Mimi. *Help for the Struggling Student: Ready-to-Use Strategies and Lessons to Build Attention, Memory, and Organizational Skills.* San Francisco, CA: Jossey-Bass, 2003.

Goleman, Daniel. *Emotional Intelligence: A New Vision for Educators* (Video). Port Chester, NY: National Professional Resources, Inc., 1996.

Goleman, Daniel. *Emotional Intelligence: Why It Can Matter More Than IQ.* New York, NY: Bantam Books, 1995.

Gore, M.C. *Successful Inclusion Strategies for Secondary and Middle School Teachers: Keys to Help Struggling Learners Access the Curriculum.* Thousand Oaks, CA: Corwin Press, 2003.

Gregory, Gale & Carolyn Chapman. *Differentiated Instructional Strategies: One Size Doesn't Fit All.* Thousand Oaks, CA: Corwin Press, 2002.

Gusman, Jo. *Differentiated Instruction & the English Language Learner: Best Practices to Use With Your Students (K-12)* (Video). Port Chester, NY: National Professional Resources, Inc., 2004.

Halvorsen, Ann T. & Thomas Neary. *Building Inclusive Schools: Tools and Strategies for Success.* Boston, MA: Allyn & Bacon, 2009.

Hannell, Glynis. *Identifying Children with Special Needs.* Thousand Oaks, CA: Corwin Press, 2005.

HBO (Producer). *Educating Peter* (Video). New York, NY: 1993.

Heacox, Diane. *Differentiated Instruction: How to Reach and Teach All Learners (Grades 3–12).* Minneapolis, MN: Free Spirit Press, 2002.

Hehir, Thomas. *New Directions in Special Education.* Cambridge, MA: Harvard University Press, 2005.

Iervolino, Constance & Helene Hanson. *Differentiated Instructional Practice Video Series: A Focus on Inclusion (Tape 1), A Focus on the Gifted (Tape 2).* Port Chester, NY: National Professional Resources, Inc. 2003.

Janney, Rachel & Martha E. Snell. *Behavioral Support: Teachers' Guides to Inclusive Practices.* Baltimore, MD: Paul H. Brookes Publishing Co., Inc., 2000.

Janney, Rachel & Martha E. Snell. *Collaborative Teaming: Teachers' Guides to Inclusive Practices.* Baltimore, MD: Brookes Publishing Company, 2000.

Janney, Rachel & Martha E. Snell. *Modifying Schoolwork: Teachers' Guides to Inclusive Practices, 2nd Edition.* Baltimore, MD: Paul H. Brookes Publishing Co., Inc., 2004.

Jensen, Eric. *The Fragile Brain: What Impairs Learning and What We Can Do About It* (DVD). Port Chester, NY: National Professional Resources, Inc., 2000.

Jensen, Eric. *Practical Applications of -Brain--Based Learning* (DVD).. Port Chester, NY: National Professional Resources, Inc., 2000.

Jorgensen, C., Nisbet, J.A., and Schuh, Mary C. *The Inclusion Facilitators Guide*. San Francisco, CA: Paul H. Brookes Publishing Co., 2005.

Kagan, Spencer & Miguel Kagan. *Multiple Intelligences: The Complete MI Book*. San Clemente, CA: Kagan Cooperative Learning, 1998.

Kame'enui, Edward J. & Deborah C. Simmons. *Adapting Curricular Materials, Volume 1: An Overview of Materials Adaptations—Toward Successful Inclusion of Students with Disabilities: The Architecture of Instruction*. Reston, VA: Council for Exceptional Children, 1999.

Karten, Toby J. *Inclusion Strategies and Interventions*. Bloomington, IN. Solution Tree Press, 2011.

Karten, Toby J. *Inclusion Strategies That Work!: Research-Based Methods for the Classroom*. Thousand Oaks, CA: Corwin Press, 2004.

Karten, Toby. *Inclusion Succeeds with Effective Strategies* (laminated reference guide). Port Chester, NY: Dude Publishing, 2009.

Katzman, Lauren I. & Allison G. Gandhi (Editors). *Special Education for a New Century*. Cambridge, MA: Harvard Educational Review, 2005.

Kemp, K.A. *Peer to Peer Instruction in the Classroom* (laminated reference guide). Port Chester, NY Dude Publishing, 2009.

Kemp, Karen & Mary Ann Eaton. *RTI: The Classroom Connection*. Port Chester, NY: Dude Publishing, 2008.

Kennedy, Craig H. & Douglas Fisher. *Inclusive Middle Schools*. Baltimore, MD: Paul H. Brookes Publishing, 2001.

Kennedy, Eugene. *Raising Test Scores for All Students: An Administrator's Guide to Improving Standardized Test Performance*. Thousand Oaks, CA: Corwin Press, 2003.

Kluth, Paula, Diana M. Straut & Douglas P. Biklen. *Access to Academics for All Students: Critical Approaches to Inclusive Curriculum, Instruction, and Policy*. Mahwah, NJ: Lawrence Erlbaum Associates, Inc., 2003.

Koegel, Lynn Kern, Robert Koegel & Glen Dunlap (Editors). *Positive Behavioral Support: Including People with Difficult Behavior in the Community*. Baltimore, MD: Brookes Publishing Company, Inc., 1996.

Kohn, Alfie. *The Schools Our Children Deserve*. New York, NY: Houghton Mifflin Company. 1999.

Kugelmass, Judy W. *The Inclusive School: Sustaining Equity and Standards*. New York, NY: Teachers College Press, 2004.

Lavoie, Richard. *Beyond F.A.T. City* (Video). Charlotte, NC: PBS Video, 2005.

Lavoie, Richard. *F.A.T. City: How Difficult Can This Be?* (Video). Charlotte, NC: PBS Video, 1989.

Levine, Mel. *A Mind at a Time.* New York, NY: Simon & Schuster, 2002.

Lickona, Thomas. *Character Matters.* New York, NY: Touchstone, 2004.

Lickona, Thomas. *Educating for Character: How Our Schools Can Teach Respect and Responsibility.* New York, NY: Bantam, 1992.

Lipsky, Dorothy K. & Alan Gartner. *Inclusion: A Service, Not A Place—A Whole School Approach* (DVD). Port Chester, NY: National Professional Resources, Inc., 2002.

Lipsky, Dorothy K. & Alan Gartner. *Inclusion and School Reform: Transforming America's -Classrooms.* Baltimore, MD: Paul H. Brookes Publishing, 1997.

Lipsky, Dorothy K. & Alan Gartner. *Standards & Inclusion: Can We Have Both?* (Video). Port Chester, NY: National Professional Resources, Inc., 1998.

Long, Nicholas, & William Morse. *Conflict in the Classroom: The Education of At-Risk and Troubled Students, 5th Edition.* Austin, TX: Pro-Ed, Inc., 1996.

Maanum, Jody L. *The General Educator's Guide to Special Education, 2nd Edition.* Minnetonka, MN: Peytral Publications, Inc., 2003.

Mather, Nancy & Sam Goldstein. *Learning Disabilities and Challenging Behaviors: A Guide to Intervention and Classroom Management.* Baltimore, MD: Brookes Publishing Company, 2001.

Maurer, Marvin & Marc Brackett. *Emotional Literacy in the Middle School.* Port Chester, NY: Dude Publishing, 2004.

McCarney, Stephen B. *The Pre-Referral Intervention Manual.* Columbia, MO: Hawthorne Educational Services, 1993.

McNary, Sarah J., Neal A. Glasgow & Cathy D. Hicks. *What Successful Teachers Do in Inclusive Classrooms: 60 Research-Based Teaching Strategies That Special Learners Succeed.* Thousand Oaks, CA: Corwin Press, 2005.

McPartland, Pat. *Implementing Ongoing Transition Plans for the IEP: A Student-Driven Approach to IDEA Mandates.* Verona, WI: Attainment Company, Inc., 2005.

Minskoff, Esther & David Allsopp. *Academic Success Strategies for Adolescents with Learning Disabilities & ADHD.* Baltimore, MD: Paul H. Brookes Publishing, 2002.

Moll, Anne M. *Differentiated Instruction Guide for Inclusive Teaching.* Port Chester, NY: Dude Publishing, 2003.

Munk, Dennis D. *Solving the Grading Puzzle for Students with Disabilities.* Whitefish Bay, WI: Knowledge by Design, Inc., 2003.

National Association of State Directors of Special Education (NASDSE). *Response to Intervention: Policy, Considerations, and Implementation.* Alexandria, VA: NASDSE, 2005.

Norlander, Karen. *RTI Tackles the LD Explosion: A Good IDEA Becomes Law* (DVD). Port Chester, NY: National Professional Resources, Inc., 2006.

Norlander, Karen. *What Educators and Parents Need to Know about Special Education* (laminated reference guide). Port Chester, NY Dude Publishing, 2009.

Pierangelo, Roger. *Special Educator's Book of Lists, 2nd Edition.* West Nyack, NY: Center for Applied Research in Education, 2003.

Purcell, Sherry & Debbie Grant. *Using Assistive Technology to Meet Literacy Standards.* Verona, WI: IEP Resources, 2004.

Reider, Barbara. *Teach More and Discipline Less.* Thousand Oaks, CA: Corwin Press, 2005.

Reiff, Henry. *Self-Advocacy Skills for Students with Learning Disabilities: Making it Happen in College and Beyond.* Port Chester, NY: Dude Publishing, 2007.

Renzulli, Joseph S. *Developing the Gifts and Talents of ALL Students: The Schoolwide Enrichment Model* (Video). Port Chester, NY: National Professional Resources, Inc., 1999.

Repp, A. C. & R. H. Horner (Editors). *Functional Analyses of Problem Behavior: From Effective Assessment to Effective Support.* Belmont, CA: Wadsworth, 1999.

Rief, Sandra F. *ADHD & LD: Powerful Teaching Strategies & Accommodations* (Video). Port Chester, NY: National Professional Resources, Inc., 2004.

Rief, Sandra F. & Julie A. Heimburge. *How to Reach & Teach All Students in the Inclusive Classroom: Ready-To-Use Strategies, Lessons, and Activities for Teaching Students with Learning Needs.* West Nyack, NY: Center for Applied Research in Education, 1996.

Rief, Sandra. *Section 504: Classroom Accommodations* (laminated reference guide). Port Chester, Dude Publishing, 2011.

Robinson, Viviane & Mei K. Lai. *Practitioner Research for Educators.* Thousand Oaks, CA: Corwin Press, 2006.

Rose, D. & A. Meyer (Editors). *Teaching Every Student in the Digital Age.* Alexandria, VA: ASCD, 2002.

Rose, D. & A. Meyer (Editors). *The Universally Designed Classroom: Accessible Curriculum and Digital Technologies.* Cambridge, MA: Harvard University Press, 2005.

Rutherford, Paula. *Instruction for All Students.* Alexandria, VA: Just Ask Publications, 2002.

Sailor, Wayne. *Creating A Unified System: Integrating General and Special Education for the Benefit of All Students* (Video). Bloomington, IN: Forum on Education, 2004.

Sailor, Wayne. *Whole-School Success and Inclusive Education: Building Partnerships for Learning, Achievement, and Accountability.* New York, NY: Teachers College Press, 2002.

Salovey, Peter. *Optimizing Intelligences: Thinking, Emotion, and Creativity* (Video). Port Chester, NY: National Professional Resources, Inc., 1998.

Sapon-Shevin, Mara. *Because We Can Change the World: A Practical Guide to Building Cooperative, Inclusive Classroom Communities.* Boston, MA: Allyn & Bacon, 1999.

Sapon-Shevin, M. *Widening the Circle: The Power of Inclusive Classrooms.* Boston, MA: Houghton Mifflin, 2007.

Sax, Caren L. & Colleen A. Thoma. *Transition Assessment: Wise Practices for Quality Lives.* Baltimore, MD: Brookes Publishing Company, 2002.

Schwarz, Shelley Peterman & Nancy Kruschke McKinney. *Organizing your IEPs.* Verona, WI: Attainment Company, Inc., 2005.

Shaywitz, Sally. *Overcoming Dyslexia: A New and Complete Science-Based Program for Reading Problems at Any Level.* New York, NY: Knopf Publishing, 2003.

Shore, Kenneth. *The ABCs of Bullying Prevention.* Port Chester, NY: Dude Publishing, 2005.

Snell, Martha E. & Rachel Janney. *Collaborative Teaming.* Baltimore, MD: Paul H. Brookes Publishing Co., Inc., 2000.

Snell, Martha E. & Rachel Janney. *Social Relationships & Peer Support.* Baltimore, MD: Paul H. Brookes Publishing Co., Inc., 2000.

Snell, Martha E. & Rachel Janney. *Teachers' Guides to Inclusive Practices.* Baltimore, MD: Brookes Publishing Company, Inc., 2000.

Sousa, David A. *How the Special Needs Brain Learns.* Thousand Oaks, CA: Corwin Press, 2001.

Stirling, Diane, G. Archibald, L. McKay & S. Berg. *Character Education Connections for School, Home and Community: A Guide for Integrating Character Education.* Port Chester, NY: National Professional Resources, Inc., 2001.

Thompson, Sandra, Rachel Quenemeen, Martha Thurlow, & James Ysseldyke. *Alternate Assessments for Students with Disabilities.* Thousand Oaks, CA: Corwin Press, 2001.

Thousand, Jacqueline S., Richard A. Villa & Ann I. Nevin. *Creativity and Collaborative Learning: The Practical Guide to Empowering Students, Teachers, and Families, 2nd Edition.* Baltimore, MD: Paul H. Brookes Publishing, 2002.

Thurlow, Martha L., Judy L. Elliott & James E. Ysseldyke. *Testing Students with Disabilities: Practical Strategies for Complying With District and State Requirements.* Thousand Oaks, CA: Corwin Press, 1998.

Tilton, Linda. *Teacher's Toolbox for Differentiating Instruction: 700 Strategies, Tips, Tools, & Techniques.* Shorewood, MN: Covington Cove Publications, 2003.

Tomlinson, Carol Ann. *How to Differentiate Instruction in Mixed-Ability Classrooms, 2nd Edition.* Alexandria, VA: ASCD, 2001.

Twachtman-Cullen, Diane & Jennifer Twachtman-Reilly. *How Well Does Your IEP Measure Up?: Quality Indicators for Effective Service Delivery.* Higganum, CT: Starfish Specialty Press, 2002.

Villa, Richard A. *Collaboration for Inclusion Video Series* (Video Set). Port Chester, NY: National Professional Resources, Inc. 2002.

Villa, Richard A. & Jacqueline S. Thousand. *A Guide to Co-Teaching.* Thousand Oaks, CA: Corwin Press, 2004.

Villa, J., and Thousand, J., and Nevin,, A.I. *Co-Teaching at a Glance* (laminated reference guide). Port Chester, NY, 2009.

Villa, Richard A. & Jacqueline S. Thousand. *Creating An Inclusive School, 2nd Edition.* Alexandria, VA: Association for Supervision & Curriculum Development, 2005.

Villa, Richard A. & Jacqueline S. Thousand. *Restructuring for Caring and Effective Education: Piecing the Puzzle Together, 2nd Edition.* Baltimore, MD: Paul H. Brookes Publishing, 2000.

Villa, J. and Thousand, J. *RTI: Co-Teaching and Differentiated Instruction* (laminated reference guide). Port Chester, NY, 2011.

Watson, T. Steuart & Mark W. Steege. *Conducting School-Based Functional Behavioral Assessments: A Practitioner's Guide.* New York, NY: Guilford Press, 2003.

Wood, M. Mary & Nicholas Long. *Life Space Intervention: Talking with Children and Youth in Crisis.* Austin, TX: -Pro--Ed, Inc., 1991.

Wright, J. *RTI and Classroom Behavior* (laminated reference guide). Port Chester, NY: Dude Publishing, 2011.

Wright, Jim. *RTI Toolkit: A Practical Guide for Schools.* Port Chester, NY: Dude Publishing, 2007.

Wright, Peter W. D., Pamela Darr Wright & Suzanne Whitney Heath. *Wrightslaw: No Child Left Behind.* Hartfield, VA: Harbor House Law Press, Inc., 2003.

Wunderlich, Kathy C. *The Teacher's Guide to Behavioral Interventions.* Columbia, MO: Hawthorne Educational Services, Inc., 1988.

Organizations and Agencies

American Association on Intellectual and Developmental Disabilities
444 North Capital Street, NW
Washington, DC 20001
(800) 424–3688
www.aamr.org

American Speech-Language Hearing Association (ASHA)
10801 Rockville Peak
Rockville, MD 20852
(800) 638–8255
www.asha.org

ARC of the United States
101 Wayne Avenue
Silver Spring, MD 20910
(301) 565–3842
www.thearc.org

Association for Supervision and Curriculum Development (ASCD)
1703 N. Beauregard Street
Alexandria, VA 22311–1714
(800) 933–2723
www.ascd.org

Autism Society of America
7910 Woodmont Avenue
Bethesda, MD 20814
(800) 328–8476
www.autism-society.org

Center for Applied Special Technology (CAST)
40 Harvard Mills Square, Suite 3
Wakefield, MA 01880
(781) 245–2212
www.CAST.org

Council for Exceptional Children (CEC)
1920 Association Drive
Reston, VA 20191–1589
(888) 232–7738
www.CEC.sped.org

Exceptional Parent
555 Kinderkamack Road
Oradell, NJ 07649–1517
(201) 634–6550
www.eparent.com

Institute on Community Integration
University of Minnesota
102 Peddee Hall
150 Pillsbury Drive, SE
Minneapolis, MN 55455
(612) 624- 6300
www.ici.umn.edu

Learning Disabilities Association of America
4156 Library Road
Pittsburgh, PA 15234
(888) 239–1946
www.LDAAmerica.org

National Association of State Directors of Special Education, Inc. (NASDSE)
1800 Diagonal Road, Suite 320
Alexandria, VA 22314
(703) 519–3800
www.nasdse.org

National Association of Elementary School Principals (NAESP)
1615 Duke Street
Alexandria, VA 22314
(800) 38-NAESP
www.naesp.org

National Association of Secondary School Principals (NASSP)
1904 Association Drive
Reston, VA 20191–1537
(703) 860–0200
www.nassp.org

National Association of the Deaf
814 Thayer Avenue
Silver Springs, MD 20910
(301) 587–1788
www.nad.org

Center for Educational Restructuring and Inclusion (CERI)
Affiliated with The Graduate School and University Center,
The City University of New York
365 Fifth Avenue
New York, NY 10016
(646) 229–4985
www.gc.cuny.edu/other_programs/research_centers_pages/NCERI.htm

National Center for Learning Disabilities
381 Park Avenue South
New York, NY 10016
(212) 545–7510
www.ncld.org

National Down Syndrome Congress
7000 Peachtree-Dunwood Road
Atlanta, GA 30328
(800) 232-6372
www.ndscenter.org

National Federation of the Blind
1800 Johnson Street
Baltimore, MD 21230
(410) 569-9314
www.nfb.org

National Information Center for Children and Youth with Disabilities (NICHYCY)
PO Box 1492
Washington, DC 20013
(800) 695-0285
www.nichcy.org

National Organization on Disability (NOD)
910 16th Street, NW
Washington, DC 20006
www.nod.org

Special Education Resource Center (SERC)
25 Industrial Park Road
Middletown, CT 06457
(860) 632-1485
www.ctserc.org

Spina Bifida Association of America
4590 MacArthur Boulevard, NW
Washington, DC 20007-4226
(202) 944-3286
www.sbaa.org

TASH
29 West Susquehanna Avenue
Baltimore, MD 21204
(410) 828-8274
www.tash.org

United Cerebral Palsy Association
1660 L Street, NW
Washington, DC 20036
(800) 872-5827
www.ucp.org

Glossary of Terms

Accommodations: Changes in format, response, setting, timing, or scheduling that do not alter in a significant way what the test measures or the comparability of scores. Sometimes used interchangeably with modifications, see below.

Adaptations: a general term which in instruction refers to supplemental aids and services, and in assessment refers to accommodations and modifications.

Adequate Yearly Progress (AYP): the improvement which states, districts, and schools must make annually, as measured by formal assessment.

Americans with Disabilities Act (ADA): Passed in 1990, this federal law provides civil rights protection for persons with disabilities; requires employers and businesses offering public accommodations to make them accessible to persons with disabilities; prohibits discrimination in employment; requires access in communication systems; requires schools to ensure that discrimination based upon disabilities doe not occur.

Alternate assessment: determination by the IEP Team that a student will not participate in a particular state- or district-wide assessment (or part of such an assessment). The IEP must include a statement of why that assessment is not appropriate for the child and how the child will be assessed. For such students, alternate assessments are to be used.

Assessment: an organized, structured way to gather information; can be used for a variety of purposes, including determination of eligibility for a child with a disability.

Attention Deficit Disorder (ADD): A condition in which a student has difficulties in directing or maintaining attention to normal tasks of learning.

Attention Deficit Hyperactivity Disorder (ADHD): A condition in which a student has significant difficulties in focusing and sustaining attention, impulsiveness, and regulation activity level.

Authentic assessment: An evaluation of a student's performance, with meaningful tasks related directly to the curriculum taught.

Behavior intervention plan (BIP): Required per the reauthorized IDEA for students whose behavior triggers special attention, per a functional behavior assessment (FBA, see below.)

Block scheduling: Scheduling for longer than the usual 45 to 50 minute periods; usually used in order to allow for the integration of curricula areas, e.g., literacy and social studies, mathematics and science, etc.

Collaboration: A team effort involving two or more adults working together and providing mutual support for each other.

Cooperative learning: A group of students with diverse skills and traits working together. This promotes collaboration, teamwork, and an appreciation of differences while fostering long-term relationships. (See Chapter 6.)

Co-teaching (or collaborative teaching): A strategy in which a general education teacher and a special education teacher plan and work together and jointly teach students in an inclusive environment. (See Chapter 4 for a description of various co-teaching models.)

Common Core State Standards: A voluntary agreement now adopted by nearly all states establishing new and more rigorous tandards in math and Language Arts. State assessments will align to the new standards by common assessments, development by one of two national consortia.

Curriculum-based assessment: The evaluation of student performance per the curriculum being taught.

Differentiated instruction: An instruction system where the teacher uses various approaches to content, process, and product in recognition of learners' differing degrees of readiness, divergent interests, and learning needs. (See Chapter 5 on differentiated classrooms.)

Disability: Impairment of normal functioning in one or more major life activities, as reinforced in Section 504 and ADA.

Free Appropriate Public Education (FAPE): The guarantee per the federal law (IDEA) for all students with disabilities to receive special education/related services as per the IEP.

Functional assessment: The assessment of student outcomes related to living and working in the community. Usually refers to students with more significant impairments.

Functional behavior assessment (FBA): Per the reauthorized IDEA, a systematic study of a student's behavior, precedent to the development of a behavior intervention plan (BIP), see above.

General education curriculum: The curriculum per each state's requirements, for students in general. Per IDEA, mastery of this curriculum, with needed supplementary aids and services, is expected for students with disabilities. The antonym to a separate special education curriculum.

Highly Qualified Teacher (HQT): teachers who are certified via a state or state exam, and who demonstrate competence in the areas they teach.

Individuals with Disabilities Education Act (IDEA): P.L. 105–17, the federal "special education" law. Reauthorized in 1997, it is the successor of P.L. 94–142, "The Education for All Handicapped Children Act," first enacted in 1975. (See Chapter 2 for a discussion of the key provisions of IDEA.)

Inclusion (inclusive education/schooling): The concept that students with disabilities, regardless of the nature and extent of their disability, should be educated with age-appropriate peers, in regular classes, with needed supplementary aids and services, in their home school. (N.B. The term does not appear in IDEA. Nor does the term "mainstreaming.")

Individualized Education Program (IEP): As required by IDEA, a written commitment on the part of the school district for the provision of services to meet the student's individual needs. The IEP includes a description of the student's current performance; measurable annual goals; required special education and related services, including needed supplementary aids and services; a description of the extent to which there is to be participation with nondisabled students; the extent to which the student is to participate in district- and state-wide assessments (along with, as necessary, needed modifications); a specification of when services will begin, where they will be provided, and how long they will last; transition services needs; and measures of progress toward the attainment of the specified goals, and when and how parents will be informed of such progress. (See Chapter 3 for a description of the IEP Team.)

Information processing: The mental manipulation of symbols, words, and perceptions to acquire knowledge and solve problems.

Learning disability (LD): A handicapping condition in which a child is achieving and performing at a level that is significantly below the expectation for her/his measured intellectual ability. The discrepancy must be due to difficulties in information processing, rather than environmental or social factors.

Learning style: The way a person organizes and responds to experiences and information.

Least Restrictive Environment (LRE): The environment in which learners with disabilities can succeed, which is most similar to the environment in which nondisabled peers are educated. Students with disabilities are to be removed from the general education setting only when the nature and severity of their disability is such that education in that setting, with supplementary aids and services, cannot be achieved satisfactorily. Although the term is not used in IDEA, it expresses the concept that students with disabilities are to be educated with their nondisabled peers, supported with needed supplementary aids and services, unless otherwise and specifically justified to the contrary. In effect, there is a presumption of inclusion.

Looping: A design wherein students are taught by the same teacher(s) for longer than one year.

Modifications: Changes in the assessment that alter what the test is to measure or the comparability of scores. Sometimes used interchangeably with accommodations, see above. More broadly, sometimes used as a synonym for adaptations made in the curriculum, presentation method, or the environment to provide support for the student with disabilities.

Natural proportion: When the number of students with disabilities in an environment reflects the percentage of individuals with disabilities generally found in the community.

Natural supports: The least-intrusive supports available in the environment in which performance is being exhibited, i.e., "less is better."

Normalization: The principle that services to people with disabilities, including children and youth, should be provided with services, including education, as similar as possible to those provided to their nondisabled peers.

Portfolio: A form of assessment involving a collection of a student's work which demonstrates what the student has learned over a period of time.

Reading: a complex system of gaining meaning from the printed word; an ability that requires mastery of a defined set of skills which include phonemic awareness, phonics, fluency, vocabulary and comprehension.

Regular education classroom: The general classroom for students in a school. Per IDEA, the presumptive location for education of students with disabilities, with needed supplementary aids and services.

Related services: Those services necessary to enable the student with disabilities to benefit from special education services. Related services include audiology, counseling, early identification and assessment, certain medical services, occupational therapy, orientation and mobility services, parent counseling and training, physical therapy, psychological services, recreation, rehabilitation counseling services, school health services, social work services in schools, speech-language pathology services, and transportation. For students with disabilities, needed related services are specified on her/his IEP.

Response to Intervention (RTI): The practice of providing high quality instruction/intervention that is matched to student needs, and using learning rate and level of performance to make important educational decisions.

Review: The IDEA requirement that a student's IEP be periodically revisited, at least once a year ("annual review") and more extensively every three years ("triennial review").

Role release: The concept that as colleagues work together they give up ("release") their sole ownership of a particular skill or area of expertise. (See Chapter 4.)

Scaffolding: Temporary and adjustable support for the development of new skills. Once mastered, the "scaffold" is "faded or dismantled.

Section 504 (of the Rehabilitation Act of 1973): A civil rights law to prohibit discrimination on the basis of disability in programs and activities, public and private, that receive federal financial assistance.

Special Education: instruction that is designed and implemented to meet the individual needs of a student with a disability.

Supplementary aids and services: Services provided on behalf of the student to implement the IEP, which may include supports for school personnel to ensure that the student benefits from special education services.

Transition services: Those services that facilitate the movement of a student with disabilities from -school--level education services to subsequent services. Per IDEA, schools must begin planning this process when the student is 14 years of age.

Universal Design for Learning (UDL): designing and delivering services and products that can be used by people with the widest possible range of functional capabilities, either with or without assistive technology; reference from the Assisted Technology Act of 1988.

Zero reject: The philosophy that no child, regardless of the nature and severity of the disability, should be excluded from school.

Endnotes

1. These categories and the percentage of the 5.2 million students, ages 6–21, served under IDEA, per the most recent report of the U.S. Department of Education, are specific learning disabilities (51.1%), speech or language impairments (20.1%), mental retardation (11.4%), emotional disturbance (8.6%), multiple disabilities (1.9%), hearing impairments (1.3%), orthopedic impairments (1.3%), other health impairments (3.1%), visual impairments (0.5%), autism (0.7%), deaf-blindness (0.1%), and traumatic brain injury (0.2%).

2. L. Fine (February 7, 2001), More students avoiding smaller 'special' buses, *Education Week,* 22(21), 1.

3. *Ibid.*

4. Adapted from *Improving education: The promise of inclusive schooling* (2000). Newton, MA: National Institute for Urban School Improvement, Education Development Center, Inc., pp. 6, f.

5. *Federal Register,* March 12, 1999.

6. The student must be invited if transition needs or services are to be discussed.

7. Cited in *A Guide to the Individualized Education Program* (July, 2000). Washington, DC: U.S. Department of Education, p. 8.

8. The material here is adapted from *Inclusion tool kit for parents: Information packet,* developed by SPAN (Statewide Parent Advocacy Network).

9. A. Hartocollis (November 22, 2000), "Teachers find toughest task is learning from each other," *New York Times,* p. B8.

10. For a wide-ranging discussion of the structure and function of teams in the middle school, see C. H. Kennedy & D. Fisher (2001), Building and using collaborative school teams, in C.H. Kennedy & D. Fisher (Eds.), *Inclusive middle schools* (pp. 27–41). Baltimore, MD: Paul H. Brookes Publishing Co. Inc.

11. S. E. Gately and F. J. Gately, Jr. (2001), Understanding coteaching components, *TEACHING Exceptional Children,* 33(4), 40–47.

12. *Ibid.,* 42.

13. The physical implication of the terms "pull out" and "push in" are contrary to the reauthorized IDEA emphasis on understanding special education as a service, not a place. Less important than where the service is provided is that the services, related and resource room, be integral with the general curriculum.

14. For a survey of such efforts, see M. F. Giangreco, P. A. Prelock, R. R. Reid, R. E. Dennis, & S. W. Edelman (2000), Roles of related services personnel in inclusive schools, in R. A. Villa & J. S. Thousand (Eds.), *Restructuring for caring and effective*

education: Piecing the puzzle together (pp. 360–388). Baltimore: Paul H. Brookes Publishing Co.

15 Gately and Gately, op cit, Figures 3 and 4.

16 C. L. Wagner & M. C. Pugach, Forming partnerships around curriculum. *Educational Leadership,* 53(5), p. 62.

17 D. H. Rose, A. Meyer, & C. Hitchcock (Eds) 2005. *The universally designed classroom: Accessible curriculum and digital technologies.* Cambridge, MA: Harvard Education Press.

18 See chapter VII.

19 See chapter VIII.

20 C. A. Tomlinson & M. L. Kalbfleisch (1998). Teach me, Teach my brain: A call for differentiated classrooms. *Educational Leadership,* 56(3), 52–55.

21 See chapter VI for a full discussion of cooperative learning.

22 See chapter VIII re. the use of technology.

23 Some school districts call this "indirect support."

24 S. K. Etscheidt & L. Bartlett (1999), The IDEA amendments: A four-step approach for determining supplementary aids and services, *Exceptional Children,* 65(2), 163–174.

25 S. Cole, B. Horvath, C. Chapman, C. Deschenes, D. G. Ebeling, & J. Sprague (2000). *Adapting curriculum and instruction in the inclusive classroom: A teacher's desk reference, 2nd ed.* Bloomington, IN: The Center for School and Community Integration, Institute for the Study of Developmental Disabilities.

26 A. Moll (2005), *Differentiated instruction guide for inclusive teaching.* Port Chester, NY: National Professional Resources, Inc.

27 M. F. Giangreco & S. W. Edelman (1995, December). Coordinating support services in inclusive classrooms. Presentation at the TASH Conference, San Francisco.

28 S. Pavri & L. Monda-Amaya (2001), Social support in inclusive schools: Student and teacher perspectives, *Exceptional Children,* 67(3), 391–411.

29 Adapted from M. Grigal (July/August, 1998). The time-space continuum: Using natural supports in inclusive classrooms. *TEACHING Exceptional Children,* 44–51.

30 J. S. Schumm, S. Vaughn, & J. Harris (1997). Pyramid power for collaborative planning. *TEACHING Exceptional Children,* 29(6), 62–66.

31 Adapted from *Curriculum accommodations and/or modifications based on Chicago academic standards* (1997). Chicago: Chicago Public Schools.

32 B. J. Scott, M. R. Vitale, & W. G. Masten (March/April, 1998), Implementing instructional adaptations for students with disabilities in inclusive classrooms, *Remedial and Special Education,* 19(2), 106–119.

33 *Questions and answers* (2000).

34 For example, the state of Washington allows four sets of accommodations for its statewide test, Washington Assessment of Student Learning (WASL): 1. *aids,* provide English, visual, or native language dictionaries, except on reading test; physical supports and assists; isolate portion of the test; clarify directions; 2. *scribe,* answer orally, point, use voice recognition technology, sign an answer, use a word processor, dictate to a scribe; 3. *large print or Braille;* and 4. *oral presentation* (e.g., read the math items verbatim in English). E. Johnson, K. Kimball, S. O. Brown, & D. Anderson (Winter 2001), A statewide review of the use of accommodations in large-scale, high-stakes assessments, *Exceptional Children* 67(2), 251–164.

35 C. A. Tomlinson (2001), Grading for success, *Educational Leadership,* 12–15.

36 Suggested here is a dual system: grades, one reflecting individual growth, e.g. "A" (excellent growth) through "F" (no observable growth), and the other relative standing, e.g., "1" (student is working above grade level in the subject) to "3" (student is working below grade level in the subject). Thus, a grade of B2 in science means that the student is making good growth and is working at grade level.

37 S. J. Salend (1998), *Effective mainstreaming: Creating inclusive classrooms.* Columbus, OH:Prentice Hall.

38 M. Sapon-Shevin, B. L. Ayres, & J. Duncan. Cooperative learning and inclusion. In J. S. Thousand, R. A. Villa, & A. I. Nevins (Eds.), *Creativity and collaborative learning: A practical guide to empowering students and teachers* (pp. 275–291). Baltimore: Paul H. Brookes Publishing Co.

39 S. Kagan (1989). The structural approach to cooperative learning. *Educational Leadership,* 47(4), 12–15.

40 See "Special series: Advances in peer-mediated instruction and interventions in the 21st century," *Remedial and Special Education* (January/February, 2001), 22(1), 2–47.

41 C. A. Utley (January/February, 2001), Introduction to the Special Series: Advances in Peer-Mediated Instruction and Interventions in the 21st Century, *Remedial and Special Education,* 22(1), 2.

42 L. Maheady, G. F. Harper, & B. Mallette (1991). Peer-mediated instruction: A review of potential applications for special education. *Reading, Writing and Learning Disabilities International,* 7, 75–103. C. A. Utley, S. L. Mortweet, & C. R. Greenwood (1997). Peer-mediated instruction and interventions. *Focus on Exceptional Children,* 29(5), 1–23.

43 L. Maheady, G. T. Harper, & B., Malette. (2001). Peer-mediated instruction and interventions and students with mild disabilities. *Remedial and Special Education,* 22(1), 7.

44 *Ibid.,* 7, f.
45 See also, C. R. Greenwood, C. Arreaga-Mayer, C. A. Utley, K. M. Gavin, & B. J. Terry. (2001). ClassWide Peer Tutoring learning management system. *Remedial and Special Education,* 22(1), 34–47.
46 See also, D. Fuchs, L. S. Fuchs, A. Thompson, E. Svenson, L. Yen, S. A. Otaiba, N. Yang, K. N. McMaster, K. Prentice, S. Kazdan, and L. Saenz. (2001). Peer-Assisted Learning Strategies in reading. *Remedial and Special Education,* 22(1), 15–21.
47 *Ibid.,* 8, ff.
48 B. Elbaum, S. Vaughn, M. Hughes, & S. W. Moody (1999). Grouping practices and reading outcomes for students with disabilities. *Exceptional Children,* 65(3), 399–415.
49 D. K. Lipsky and A. Gartner (1987). Capable of achievement and worthy of respect: Education of the handicapped as if they were full fledged human beings. *Exceptional Children,* 54(1), 69–76.
50 A. Gartner & D. K. Lipsky (1990). Students as instructional agents. In W. Stainback & S. Stainback (Eds.), *Support networks for inclusive schooling: Interdependent integrated education* (pp. 81–98). Baltimore: Paul H. Brookes Publishing Co.
51 B. Burrell, S. J. Wood, T. Pikes, & C. Holliday (Jan/Feb, 2001), Student mentors and proteges learning together, *TEACHING Exceptional Children,* 33(3), 24–29.
52 W. Damon (1984). Peer education: The untapped potential. *Journal of Applied Developmental Psychology,* 5, 331–343.
53 Big kids teach little kids: What we know about cross aged tutoring. (1987). *Harvard Education Letter,* 3(2), 2.
54 A. Gartner, M. K. Kohler, F. Riessman (1971). *Children teach children: Learning through teaching.* New York: Harper & Row.
55 A. Gartner & D. K. Lipsky, *op cit.*
56 Handicapped children as tutors. (1984). Salt Lake City, UT: David O. McKay Institute of Education, Brigham Young University.
57 *National study of inclusive education* (2nd ed.) (1995). New York: National Center on Educational Restructuring and Inclusion, pp. 158, ff.
58 N. Schniewind & E. Davidson (September 2000), *Differentiating cooperative learning. Educational Leadership,* 58(1), 25.
59 M. Elias, L. B. Butler (2005). *Social decision making/social problem solving: A curriculum for academic, social and emotional learning.* Champaign, FL: Research Press.
60 L. Fine (2001). IDEA doesn't hinder discipline, survey finds. *Education Week* (February 7), 6.
61 *Ibid.*

62 At the end of the chapter, we excerpt from *Prevention Research & the IDEA Discipline Provisions: A Guide for School Administrators,* transmitted by Judith E. Heumann, Assistant Secretary, Office of Special Education and Rehabilitative Services, and Kenneth Warlick, Director, Office of Special Education Programs, US Department of Education, January 2001.

63 L. M. Bambara & T. Knoster (1998). *Designing positive behavior support plans.* Washington, DC: American Association on Mental Retardation, p. 5. Reprinted with permission.

64 Excepted from L. M. Bambara & T. Knoster (1998), *Designing positive behavior support plans.* Washington, DC: American Association on Mental Retardation, Table 4. Reprinted with permission.

65 Bambara & Knoster, Table 6. Reprinted with permission.

66 In the largest gift to a public university, $250 million has been donated to the University of Colorado to establish a center for research on technological advances that would help people with cognitive disabilities.

67 J. M. Roschelle, R. D. Pea, C. M. Hoadley, D. N. Gordon, & B. M. Means (Fall/Winter 2000), Changing how and what children learn in school with computer-based technologies, *The Future of Children,* 10(2), 76–101.

68 This is the formulation of Pressman and Blackstone (1997).

69 Developed by the Center for Applied Special Technology (CAST), Peabody, MA.